Ultimate Mustang /
629 COV

48710

P9-CJM-077

Covert, Pat.
Sheridan County Library

4/05

DATE DUE

JUL 5 - 2005		
MAY 1 4 2012		
AUG 1 5 2016		
	DEMCO 128-5046	

Ultimate
MUSTANG

Ultimate
MUSTANG

PATRICK COVERT
with
William Bozgan

DK

LONDON, NEW YORK, MELBOURNE, DELHI,
and MUNICH

Senior Editor Jill Hamilton
Publisher Sean Moore
Art Director Tina Vaughan
Production Manager Chris Avgherinos

Designed and developed by
Southern Lights Custom Publishing

Project Director Tim Kolankiewicz
Managing Editor Shelley DeLuca
Production Director Lee Howard
President Ellen Sullivan
Additional Design Miles Parsons, Scott Fuller

First North American Edition, 2001

03 04 05 10 9 8 7 6 5 4 3

Published in the United States by
DK Publishing, Inc.
375 Hudson Street
New York, NY 10014

Copyright © 2002 DK Publishing, Inc.

All rights reserved under International and Pan-American
Copyright Conventions. No part of this publication may be
reproduced, stored in a retrieval system, or transmitted in any
form or by any means, electronic, mechanical,
photocopying, recording, or otherwise, without the prior
written permission of the copyright owner.

DK Publishing offers special discounts for bulk purchases for
sales promotions or premiums. Specific, large-quantity needs
can be met with special editions, including personalized covers,
excerpts of existing guides, and corporate imprints. For more
information, contact Special Markets Department,
DK Publishing, Inc., 375 Hudson Street, New York, NY 10014
Fax: 212-689-5254.

Library of Congress Cataloging-in-Publication Data

Covert, Pat.
  Ultimate Mustang / Patrick Covert.
    p. cm.
  Includes index.
  ISBN 0-7894-6244-3 (alk. paper)
  1. Mustang automobile.   I. Title.
TL215.M8 C69 2001
629.222'2—dc21
                                              00-065936

Printed and bound in the United States
by Quebecor, Taunton, Massachusetts

Contents

Foreword 6
Introduction 8

Foreword

ALMOST 37 YEARS AGO, Ford launched the Mustang and started something special in the auto industry – certainly something very special for Ford. It was a new breed of car, one that created an exciting new category popularly known as "pony cars." In the auto industry, introductions like the Mustang launch in April of 1964 do not happen very often. That level of interest and excitement – the Mustang mania, as it may be called – is a rare phenomenon. From its first public unveiling in 1964 at the New York World's Fair, Mustang has become an American legend. Imagine, 22,000 orders the first day the Mustang went on sale! A true testament to the Mustang's universal appeal is the fervor and loyalty the car has generated and continues to generate among its owners. Today that mystique has resulted in more than 450 Mustang owners' clubs, including nearly 100,000 members in 20 countries, even in countries where Mustangs are not sold.

IN THE LONG RUN
Ford's commitment to the Mustang nameplate, one of the longest running in automotive history, is evident in this special edition GT released in 1999 to celebrate the Mustang's 35th anniversary.

The Mustang was something new, different, the right car at the right time. From day one, Mustang was a car that meant freedom, excitement, and fun driving. Most important, these things were packaged at an affordable price. Mustang is a star that continues to bring excitement into the lives of today's buyers. It has become a part of our lives. Mustang appeal has even found its way onto the silver screen in movies such as *Goldfinger*, *Diamonds are Forever*, *Bullitt*, *Starman*, and *Bull Durham*. As a brand, Mustang is one of Ford's strongest and most enduring; and what that brand promises has stayed the course for 37 years. Mustang is all about fun, free spirit, and feeling youthful. It appeals to all kinds of drivers – young and old alike. Coupe or convertible, V-6 or V-8, there is no singular Mustang customer. One thing for certain, the Mach, Boss, Cobra, and the GT performance models have always cast an inspirational glow over the entire Mustang family.

Janine Bay

Janine Bay
Director, Global Vehicle Personalization
Ford Motor Company

An American Phenomenon

Ford Motor Company has always been one of the most influential carmakers in the world. Starting with the introduction of the Model T Ford in 1917, Ford has stood at the forefront of innovation and customer service. Ford had the resources needed to out-research, out-develop, and out-produce General Motors and Chrysler in the 1960s, and took full advantage of its posture in the market to launch the new Ford Mustang. Never before or since has an American car had a launching as successful as the one that occurred on April 17, 1964. That day marked the world's first look at the Mustang. What would follow is one of the most unique stories in American business and cultural history.

The 1964½ Ford Mustang was the result of keen corporate insight, design ingenuity, and perfect timing. Like the introduction of any new automobile, the Mustang was a risk. Fortunately for Ford Motor Company, it was a calculated risk that would pay off for decades. For Ford and all the rest of us, Mustang would go even farther than that, transcending the world of commerce to become an icon of American life. Like fireworks on the Fourth of July, the Ford Mustang phenomenon celebrates who we are.

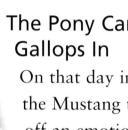

THE FAMILY THAT STARTED IT
Henry Ford I, Mrs. Henry Ford, and Henry Ford II with the first Ford automobile, the Mustang's original ancestor.

The Pony Car Gallops In

On that day in April, the Mustang touched off an emotional public response not unlike those generated earlier by Frank Sinatra, Elvis Presley, and The Beatles. One has to wonder whether Henry Ford I, visionary that he was, ever imagined that his company would produce a vehicle that would define a generation and spawn its own secondary industry of toys and specialty items. From its launch in 1964, the Mustang just seemed a natural for adaptation to everything from model car kits to toys and clothing – even golf clubs. The original 1964 dealership promotional items are highly

Ford Mustang Convertible

the unexpected...

Mustang hits
the starting line
full bore!

Here's Ford's new kind of car . . . and no car ever hit the road quite so ready for action. Mustang has a long, long list of goodies *now*, not six months or a year after introduction. Let's check down the list:

1. Three V-8's, from the supersmooth 164-hp version with hydraulic lifters through a strong 210-hp two-barrel, right up to the solid lifter-header exhaust high-performance 271-hp stormer. And that's not the end; the whole Cobra kit bolt-on array is available. (You want the four-Weber 345-

horse wild one? Just let us know.)

2. Transmissions? The V-8 choice starts with the all-synchro 3-speed manual. Or four-on-the-floor. Or Cruise-O-Matic Drive. All with floor shifts.

3. What else? A special handling package (included with high-performance V-8's) that makes the Mustang solid as a Pullman car on the corners. A Rally Pac that combines tach and clock with sweep-second hand. And, just to show we're versatile, air conditioning, a six-cylinder saver, power steering

and all the other *dolce vita* items.

We hope we're not immodest, but the Mustang four-seater starts life with the kind of equipment and options most cars take years to come by. And the kind of rock-solid handling. And the toughness and durability it takes to build a going competition machine.

Come down to your Ford Dealer's and take a long, careful look. If we've skipped anything that would make your heart glad we'd like to hear about it—but what could it be?

For a precisely detailed, authentic scale model of the new Ford Mustang, send $1.00 to Ford Offer, Department CB-1, P.O. Box 55, Troy, Michigan. (Offer ends July 31, 1964.)

TRY TOTAL PERFORMANCE FOR A CHANGE!

FORD

Mustang · Falcon · Fairlane · Ford · Thunderbird

FORD'S "NEW KIND OF CAR"

The Mustang launch is now considered a classic marketing coup. According to this ad, "no car ever hit the road so ready for action."

prized today, especially by those who remember that monumental launch day in April. Many people don't know that the Mustang's unveiling was actually trumped two weeks earlier by that of the Plymouth Barracuda. Chrysler's top executives were well aware of the development of the Mustang over a year before the new car went

into production. The Pentastar also had an "affordable sporty car" up its sleeve and rushed to blunt the debut of Ford's offering. It did Chrysler little good. The Barracuda had nowhere near the panache of the Mustang, and so successful was Ford's blitz of marketing for its little four-seater that not only would Mustang sales figures swamp its Chrysler rival, but the name "pony car" would be attributed to the Mustang and all others like it.

PEDAL CAR PROMO

The Mustang marketing blitz aimed to start Mustang owners young, with this pedal car sold at dealerships in 1964 for only $12.95.

A Winning Formula

Ironically, one of the key figures in the design and production of the Mustang was none other than Lee Iacocca, the man who would in later years pull Chrysler from utter languishment in the mid-1980s. Henry Ford II had tapped Iacocca, a brilliant young Ford marketing manager, to fill Robert McNamara's shoes as vice president and general manager in 1960, when McNamara left to join John F. Kennedy's cabinet. It was, to say the least, a good decision. Out of one of Iacocca's "little black books," in which he kept notes on new ideas, sprang the germ of

P-51 MUSTANG

The P-51, inspiration for the "Mustang" car name, was the premier US Air Force fighter-bomber throughout World War II.

the concept for the Mustang. Interestingly, the name Mustang, a high-spirited wild horse, seems like it must have been a natural for the fresh wild car Ford created. But it was the last-minute contribution of Ford executive stylist John Najjar, who had a lifelong fascination with the P-51 Mustang, one of the world's top-performing fighter aircraft prior

MASS PRODUCTION

On March 4, 1964, Mustangs began rolling off the assembly line in Dearborn, Michigan, as fast as Ford could manufacture them. Shortly thereafter, plants in San Jose, California, and Metuchen, New Jersey, were assembling the vehicles. A total of 121,538 Mustangs sold in the first 12 months of production.

to the advent of jet technology. Before Najjar thought of the Mustang name, the car was known at Ford under the code name of "T-5" or the "special Falcon" project.

The reasons for the inaugural Mustang's success were many. It was America's first affordable sporty performance car. The Chevrolet Corvette, introduced more than ten years earlier in 1953, was the country's first true sports car, but its price tag of about $3,500 – a hefty sum for an automobile at the time – precluded it from becoming a car for the masses. The Thunderbird, Ford's answer to the Corvette, was considered equally unaffordable, and three years after its introduction in 1955, the car had grown into a bloated coupe and convertible that bore very little resemblance to its former sleek self. The Mustang, at less than $2,500, flaunted a price as attractive as its appearance.

The Mustang's four-seat design also weighed into its immediate success. This was a high-spirited car the family could enjoy, the first of its type. Dad could live out his fantasies as a race car driver; Mom could enjoy sporty driving; teenagers could drive the family car and still be cool.

Racing for Success

1966 MUSTANG A/FX DRAG CAR
Fans packed the stands to see Mustang drivers such as Bill Lawton, Hubert Platt, and Al Joniec (shown here driving a Rice-Holman team car in 1966) compete to see who was the quickest at the drag strip.

Another key ingredient in the recipe for Mustang magic has been the car's leadership on the race course. From the beginning, when the Mustang was chosen to pace the 1964 Indy 500, Ford made a commitment to racing. Racing meant performance and performance meant Mustang. Thus Ford stood behind the teams campaigning Mustangs on the Trans-Am and drag racing circuits. The list of performance experts who dedicated themselves to the Mustang cause reads like a who's who of racing.

The Mustang racing hall of fame would have to include Carroll Shelby, who built and raced a new breed of Mustang; winning drivers such as Jerry Titus, George Follmer, Parnelli Jones, Dorsey Schroeder, and Tommy Kendall; Ford dealer Bob Tasca, who wouldn't rest until he'd come up with a more powerful engine; Jack Roush, who after a stellar driving and engineering career went on to oversee an unbeatable racing program at Ford; Steve Saleen, who like Shelby took a passionate vision and made it into a Mustang of beauty and performance. These are the people and cars of which American legends are made.

REBORN CLASSIC

Mustang tradition is alive and well in such classics as this 2001 fastback GT modeled after the one Steve McQueen drove in the 1968 movie *Bullitt*.

GONE TO THE RACES

Tommy Kendall dominated the Trans-Am circuit in this 1994 Mustang prepared by Jack Roush.

A Special Breed

The Ford Mustang has gone through four generations since its debut, with notable changes each time. Mustang grew larger to accept bigger engines, then was downsized to get back to its roots. The car was then "Europeanized" to compete in today's tighter markets, and updated to meet the high standards of some of the world's best sports cars. During these periods we see distinctive elements, such as the famous side scallops, come and go with the tides of change. But one thing hasn't changed. The Ford Mustang is still the most popular and

MUSTANG LOVE
When asked to choose "between a supercharger and a new kitchen floor" for her birthday, Mustang Club of America member Theresa Sanderson says she took the supercharger for her 1995 Mustang.

affordable of American sporty performance cars. Mustang people are also a special breed. They don't just like Mustangs, they love them to the extent that they will do extraordinary things to show their affection. One female Mustang owner had, in her enthusiasm, tattooed the pony-and-stripes emblem on her arm. And it was not at all uncommon as we gathered Mustangs for the photographs in this book to find that some owners had two, three, and even four more of the cars back home. Of all the Mustang owners I met, one thread ran throughout. They were all fun-loving, warm, and genuine people who would bend over backward to help. Mustang people, just like the Mustangs they own, are special.

Patrick Covert

1
THE PONY ERA BEGINS

1964½–1966

The 1964½ Ford Mustang (above and left) made sporty driving excitement accessible to more Americans than ever before. The freedom and exhilaration the Mustang symbolized, and allowed its owners to express, were unmatched. The culture of a country, and indeed the world, would never be the same.

The Mustang Arrives

APRIL 17TH 1964 ISSUE

ONE OF THE WORLD'S MOST POPULAR CARS was introduced to the public on April 17, 1964. Members of the press, invited four days earlier to view the car in the Ford Pavilion at the New York World's Fair, gathered with Henry Ford II and company executives for the unveiling of the much-anticipated Mustang. At the same time, the new car appeared on the covers of both *Time* and *Newsweek*. The night before the debut, Ford commercials promoted the car on major television networks, followed by ads in more than 2,600 newspapers. Launch weekend was a spectacular success. More than 4 million people visited dealer showrooms, and more than 22,000 cars were ordered. In one case, 15 buyers bid on a single car. Crowds threatened to stampede showrooms; a truck driver passing a dealership was so distracted he drove through the showroom window.

INSTANT SENSATION
The media frenzy surrounding the car's debut included the presentation by Tiffany's of a design award for Mustang. It was the first time the company had presented such an award for a commercial product.

Cars & Culture 1964–1966

1964: Barracuda Debuts	1964: Indy 500	1965-66: Racing
Competition was almost nonexistent when Mustang debuted. At the time, Chevrolet's Nova SS and Plymouth's Barracuda were the only sporty and affordable automobiles catching the eye of America, but they were designed to compete with Ford's compact, the Falcon.	Only a few weeks after its launch in April, 1964, the Mustang was chosen as the official pace car of the Indianapolis 500, held on Memorial Day weekend.	The first Mustangs took to the drag strip in 1965 and '66, achieving considerable success. Tasca Ford of East Providence, RI, which was among the first to campaign Mustangs at the drag strip, raced the cars in the A/FX class.

'64 Plymouth Barracuda

Mustang pace car

Mustang A/FX drag car

People Behind the Mustang

GENE BORDINAT JR.

For more than 19 years, Gene Bordinat Jr. served as vice president and director of the Ford Motor Company styling office. He was an exceptional blend of businessman and designer, measuring his success in sales as well as aesthetics. Unlike his predecessors, he believed in designing cars through teamwork and investing in resources to improve the spirit and results of cooperative design. Without a doubt his biggest hit was the 1965 Mustang.

Born in Detroit on February 10, 1920, Bordinat showed artistic talent at an early age. He graduated from high school a year early and attended the University of Michigan, followed by Harley Earle's School for Automotive Stylists. He went to work for General Motors in 1939. During World War II he helped set up the tank production line at GM's plant in Flint, Michigan, and served in the Army Air Corps. Bordinat joined Ford as an entry-level stylist in 1947.

Gene Bordinat Jr. at Ford around 1964

By 1954, he was managing Lincoln-Mercury styling. After assuming the styling vice presidency in 1961, he immediately doubled the design workspace, added two wings to the design center, and hired more staff. He put the advanced studios and fabricating shops in proximity to the design team work areas.

Bordinat ended the construction of traditional 3/8-scale clay models and focused on the exclusive use of full-size models, which became the Ford standard and are still used today. Weekly styling shows presented for Ford management were also started by Bordinat and remain an institution today.

Bordinat's vision of car design by cooperative teamwork did not always result in stellar performers on the road or on the sales books, but his approach to automotive design did produce a combination of people and ideas that resulted in some inimitable nameplates, including Mustang, Pinto, Fairmont, and Mercury Capri, to name a few.

1965: More Cars

In 1965 American automakers set a production record of 9,335,277 cars manufactured in one year – more than any other year in history and well over a million more than a decade earlier.

Ford assembly line

1965: First GT

Ford introduced the first Mustang GT models in April, 1965. Featuring a V-8 engine and racy performance and styling features, the GT package was available on any model Mustang but was especially impressive on the new fastback, also introduced in 1965.

Mustang fastback GT

1966: Mustang Sally

In 1966, rhythm and blues singer Wilson Pickett recorded what would become one of the most famous car songs in pop music. "Mustang Sally," about a woman who is too devoted to her 1965 Mustang, remains one of the most enduring songs of the 1960s and is certainly the most revered by Mustang lovers.

Wilson Pickett

The Mustang Concept

THE MUSTANG'S ORIGINS can be traced to two concept vehicles that came out of Ford's Advanced Styling Center in the early 1960s. The Mustang I was the result of then-general manager Lee Iacocca's desire that Ford produce an affordable sports car with youth appeal. The Mustang I, with its midship-mounted, four-cylinder engine and wraparound windshield, was too radical for mass production. But it inspired another styling exercise, the 1963 Mustang II show car. Ford rolled out the Mustang II for the press at Watkins Glen Raceway on the day before that year's October Grand Prix. The production Mustang that would debut a half year later owed its four-seat configuration and many of its styling cues to the Mustang II.

VERTICAL TAILLIGHTS
The vertical three-lens taillight design on the Mustang II went on to become a standard styling feature on many models.

NOTCHED REAR
The factory Mustang took its notched rear-end treatment and muscular hump of the rear fenders directly from the Mustang II

SIDE SCALLOP
The scalloped side panels on the Mustang II were carried over to the production car virtually unchanged. The chrome finger trim would appear in 1966

THE MUSTANG I CONCEPT CAR

Ford Motor Company's design engineers began work on a two-seat sports car in early 1962. One of the designers on the project, John Najjar, named the concept car Mustang after a swift, combat-worthy World War II airplane of the same name. Although originally a show car, the Mustang I was fully developed after clay models were approved. It came to life as a road-worthy, mid-engine sports car that was actually raced at several tracks across the United States, including Watkins Glen and Monterey. While the first production Mustang was not a two-seater and did not have an midship-mounted engine, several Mustang I styling ideas were carried over to the Mustang II show car and eventually to the first production vehicle.

The original Mustang I was a conceptual two-seat sports car named after the P51 Mustang, a highly regarded World War II fighter plane

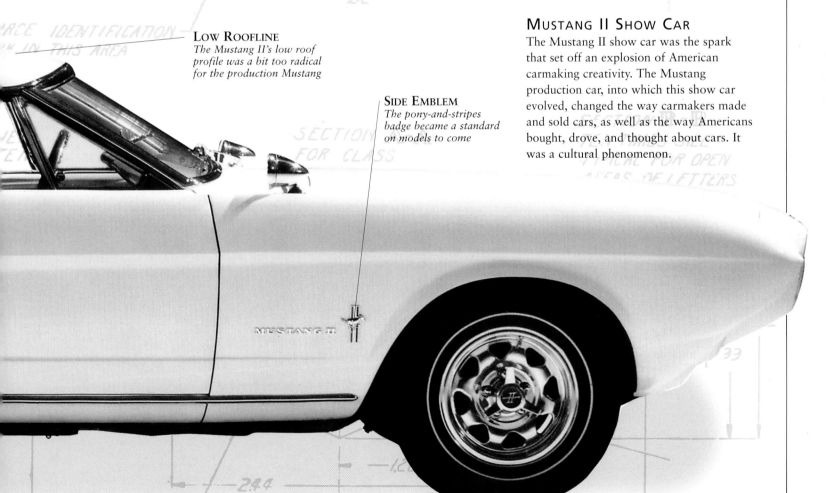

LOW ROOFLINE
The Mustang II's low roof profile was a bit too radical for the production Mustang

SIDE EMBLEM
The pony-and-stripes badge became a standard on models to come

MUSTANG II SHOW CAR

The Mustang II show car was the spark that set off an explosion of American carmaking creativity. The Mustang production car, into which this show car evolved, changed the way carmakers made and sold cars, as well as the way Americans bought, drove, and thought about cars. It was a cultural phenomenon.

1964½ Mustang Convertible

THE GALLOPING HORSE
GRILLE ORNAMENT

THE FORD MUSTANG was an instant success. In the car's first year, sales topped 417,000, shattering previous sales records of any one model in the history of the automobile. Ten months later it passed the million-unit sales mark. The Ford Mustang not only had arrived, but it also had served notice to all other auto manufacturers that a new genre of automobile, the "pony car," was carving out new trails and if you did not have one in your stable, you would be left in the dust. The Chevrolet Camaro, Pontiac Firebird, and Dodge Challenger all owe their inspiration to the darling from Dearborn, Michigan – the Mustang.

INTERIOR
A faux racing-style steering wheel added to the Mustang's exciting image as well as numerous interior options from which buyers could choose.

THE CAR THAT STARTED IT ALL
The 1964½ Mustang convertible is also known as "Early 1965." Either designation refers to models produced before August 17, 1964. Base price on this initial convertible model was only $2,368.

RAG TOP
Convertible top fabric was waterproof canvas

CONVERTIBLE BOOT
The Mustang convertible was one of two body styles offered the first year

BAGGAGE
Trunk-mounted luggage rack was an option

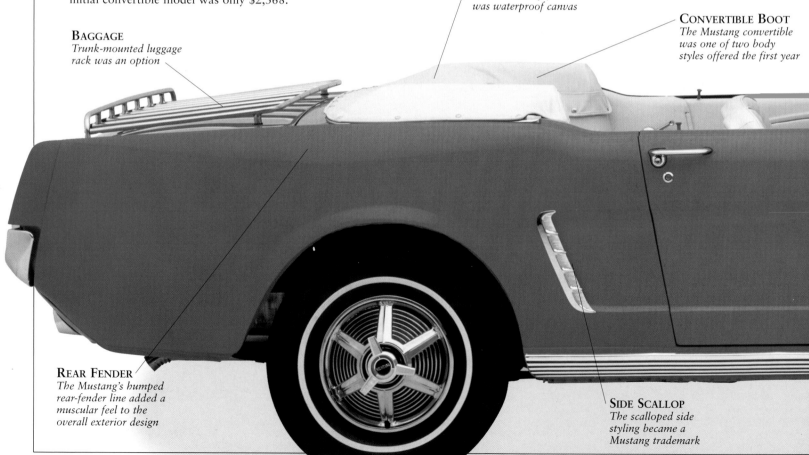

REAR FENDER
The Mustang's humped rear-fender line added a muscular feel to the overall exterior design

SIDE SCALLOP
The scalloped side styling became a Mustang trademark

THE 260 ENGINE: THE FIRST V-8

The first V-8 powerplant that Ford offered in the Mustang was a 260cid engine with a two-barrel carburetor, found only in 1964¹/₂ models. This would be the only year for a generator; Ford switched to an alternator for charging the battery for the 1965 model year.

The 260 was the first eight-cylinder engine offered with the Mustang

SPECIFICATIONS

MODEL SHOWN	**1964¹/₂ Mustang Convertible**
PRODUCTION	28,833 units
BODY STYLES 1964¹/₂–66	Convertible, coupe, fastback
CONSTRUCTION	Unibody chassis/body
ENGINES	200cid I-6 (1964¹/₂–66) 260cid V-8 (1964¹/₂) 289cid V-8 (1965–66)
POWER OUTPUT	101 hp (200cid I-6) to 271 hp (289cid V-8)
TRANSMISSION	Three- and four-speed manual or three-speed automatic
SUSPENSION	Independent front with coil springs and wishbones; semielliptic leaf springs at rear
BRAKES	Drums standard; discs optional on front
MAXIMUM SPEED	108 mph (177–204 km/h) (289cid) 0–60 mph (0–96 km/h) 8.1 seconds (289cid) 0–100 mph (0–161 km/h) 24.6 seconds (289cid) A.F.C. 16 mpg (210 hp V-8)

LOW PROFILE

The Mustang sported a low profile for its day, enhancing the sharklike fascia.

TAILLIGHTS

The early Mustang's distinctive taillights featured a modular tri-segment theme.

ENGINE IDENTIFICATION
All Mustangs with V-8s had an emblem designating the size of the engine

WINDSHIELD POST
Front windshield corner posts featured solid chrome not found on the hardtop

WHEEL COVERS
Six-spoked wheel covers with simulated knock-off hubcaps were optional

1964 Indy 500 Pace Car

THE MUSTANG RECEIVED THE HONOR of being named the official Indianapolis 500 pace car of 1964, and for the occasion Ford created a special convertible version. To take advantage of the opportunity, the company produced about 230 more pace cars – 35 were convertibles and the remainder hardtops – to promote the Mustang brand across the United States. The convertibles were sold to dealerships after the race, and the hardtops were given out in two special dealer contests in April. Convertible pace cars were equipped with 289cid engines, while the hardtop versions ran the original, less powerful 260 V-8 powerplant. Now these pace cars are highly collectible and fraudulent models have found their way into the hands of unwary buyers over the years.

RACING HEIR
Benson Ford, great-grandson of Henry Ford, poses behind the wheel of the Mustang Indy pace car on race day.

CONVERTIBLE PACE CAR
The Mustang convertible Indianapolis 500 pace car is rarer than the hardtop. Fewer were produced, and it came equipped with the larger 289 V-8 engine. Ford sold the convertibles to dealerships after the race.

UNDER THE HOOD
Convertible pace cars featured the 289 engine slated for 1965 production

INTERIOR
All pace cars came with white upholstery

FORD GOES RACING AT INDY

The Ford DOHC engine put an end to front-engine Indy 500 race cars

In the early 1960s, Ford Motor Company embarked on the most aggressive racing effort in the history of automobile manufacturing: to compete in every principal motor sports venue. Its biggest focus was perhaps the Indianapolis 500. At the time, the main racing competition in Indianapolis was front-engine race cars powered by Offenhauser engines. Dan Gurney and Colin Chapman, both veterans of the European Formula 1 racing circuit, proposed a rear-engine design powered by a fuel-injected 260 engine with dual overhead camshafts (DOHC). By 1965, the Ford-Lotus had been fully developed and took the race with driver Jimmy Clark breaking finish a full 31 seconds ahead of the pack.

Hᴀʀᴅᴛᴏᴘ Pᴀᴄᴇ Cᴀʀ

Hardtop versions of the Mustang Indianapolis 500 pace car came equipped with the original, less powerful 260 V-8 powerplants. The cars were dispersed to dealers nationwide through a contest in each of Ford's 37 sales districts.

Sᴘᴇᴄɪᴀʟ Gʀᴀᴘʜɪᴄꜱ
These commemorated the 1964 Indianapolis 500

Bᴏᴏᴛ
Convertible pace cars had a unique blue boot to cover the top when down

Pᴀɪɴᴛ
Pace cars featured Wimbledon White exteriors

Sᴛʀɪᴘᴇꜱ
Pace cars had blue stripes on the trunk and hood

PACE CAR

KEY FEATURES
1964¹/₂ Mustang Pace Car

- **Production:** 230 units (approx.)
- **First Mustang to pace the Indy 500**
- **Special stripes**
- **Dealer-installed door graphics**
- **Special engine (convertible only)**

1965 Mustang Coupe

WITH COUPE, CONVERTIBLE, and fastback models, Ford had more variations to offer the eager public. The coupe continued to be the top choice for Mustang buyers in 1965. Despite its more formal look, the coupe outsold the convertible and fastback individually five to one, accounting for nearly 75 percent of total sales for the model year. One of the coupe's biggest advantages was its price. At $2,372 suggested retail, it cost $217 less than the fastback and $242 less than the convertible. That price difference could put a V-8 engine under the hood and a sporty four-speed transmission on the floor. Then there were the utilitarian reasons for buying a Mustang coupe: The convertible was not as practical for daily driving due to weather conditions, and a fastback did not offer the convenient trunk space found in the coupe.

SPEEDOMETER
1965 was the last year for the horizontal speedometer layout derived from the Ford Falcon.

1965 COUPE, THE TOP SELLER
The hardtop continued to be the big seller; it was more practical than other models because it had a larger trunk, more rear seat room, and a classic look that appealed to more people.

WINDSHIELD
A tinted windshield with darkened top banding was optional

EDGE OF HOOD
The lead edge of the hood sides was rolled under for 1965

NEW COLOR
Honey Gold was one of five new colors added for 1965

VENT WINDOWS
Provided additional ventilation to occupants

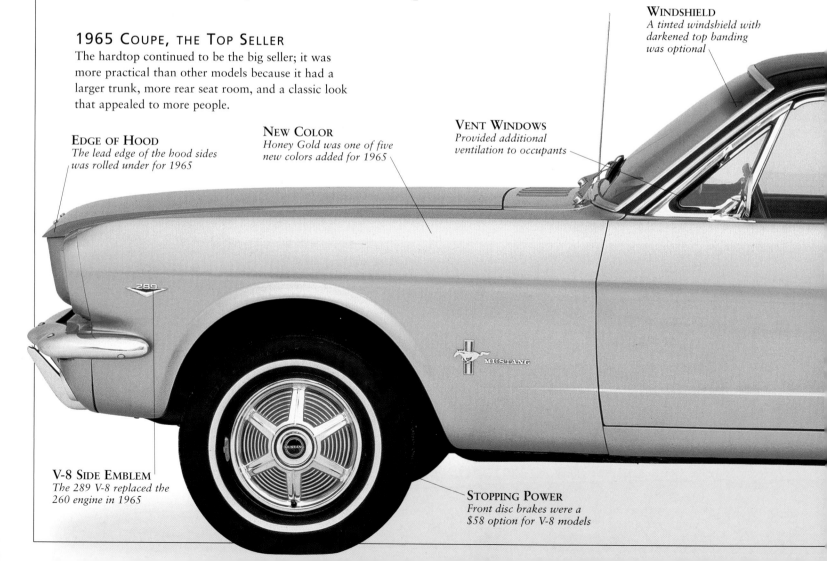

V-8 SIDE EMBLEM
The 289 V-8 replaced the 260 engine in 1965

STOPPING POWER
Front disc brakes were a $58 option for V-8 models

KEY FEATURES

1965 Mustang Coupe

- **Production:** 409,260 units
- **Leading edge of the hood corners changed slightly**
- **Modified window cranks**
- **Alternator replaced generator**

Mustang 289 V-8 emblem

THE CHALLENGER 289 V-8

The Challenger 289 V-8 could be equipped with a four-barrel carburetor as an option. The engine had a compression ratio of 10.0:1 and was rated at 225 hp. It required premium fuel. Starting in 1965, Ford replaced the generator in all Mustangs with an alternator for improved efficiency and reliability. The gold air cleaner and valve covers denote this engine as a 225-hp 289.

The Ford Mustang 289 V-8 engine

FRONT END DESIGN
Except for the front corners of the hood, which are folded under more sharply, the front end was unchanged from the 1964¹/₂ model.

TAILLIGHT DESIGN
Although the 1965 Mustang's taillights appeared to be in three sections, they were a single unit with a decorative bezel.

VINYL TOP
Vinyl top was an upscale option for the coupe

WHEEL COVER
Wheel covers were designed to give the car a sense of motion, even at a standstill

REAR END
An optional Equa-Lock limited-slip differential was available

1965 Mustang GT

THE FIRST MUSTANG GT models were introduced in April 1965. With such a premium on performance at that time, Ford believed a racier model to be a sure bet. The GT formula was simple: Equip Mustang with a feisty V-8, throw in a variety of performance features, and wrap it all up in racy cosmetics. The 1965 Mustang GT was available in all three body styles: hardtop, convertible, and 2+2 fastback. Two optional V-8 engines were offered with the GT with either 225 or 271 hp and a choice of a three- or four-speed manual, or a Cruise-O-Matic. Other performance components included heavy-duty suspension, front disc brakes, and a special dashboard instrument cluster that became standard in 1966. The GT was dressed up with stripes on the lower body sides, fog lamps, dual exhaust tips, and complementary emblems on the front fenders. The GT package was available for $165.03, an amount that cannot buy a single option today.

GT BADGE
The GT name came from the Italian term *gran tourismo,* meaning "grand touring."

FASTBACK DEBUTS
This was the first year for the fastback and for a new color, Poppy Red. The fastback would later become the basis for the groundbreaking, racy Shelby GT-350.

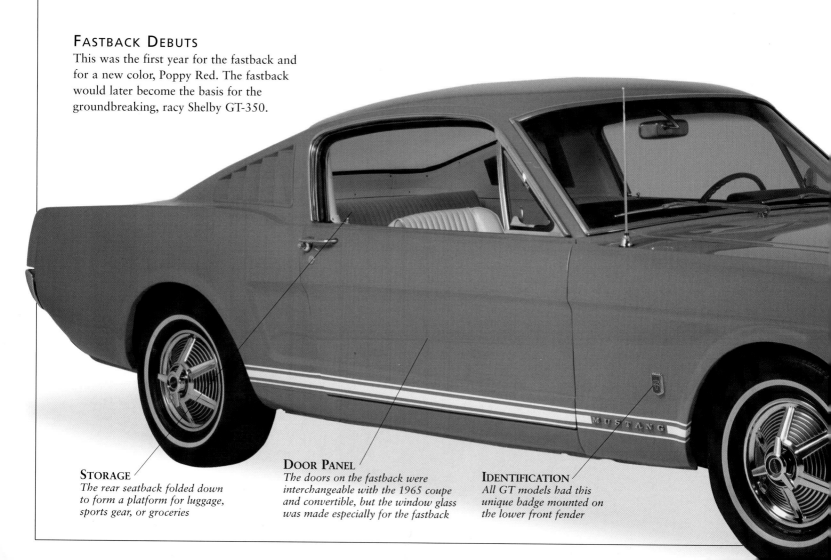

STORAGE
The rear seatback folded down to form a platform for luggage, sports gear, or groceries

DOOR PANEL
The doors on the fastback were interchangeable with the 1965 coupe and convertible, but the window glass was made especially for the fastback

IDENTIFICATION
All GT models had this unique badge mounted on the lower front fender

2+2 FASTBACK

The "2+2" was Ford's marketing tag for a two-passenger car with room for two more passengers in a fold-down rear seat.

ROOF REAR
The swooped 2+2 roofline made for a small trunk, but there was extra storage behind the rear seat

SIDE ROOF VENTS
The five vertical side vents on the fastback not only added a racy look but also were fully functional, providing air ventilation to the interior

GAS CAP
1965 GTs used the standard Mustang gas cap

DUAL EXHAUSTS
Dual exhausts, standard on the GT, exited through holes in the lower rear valance panel

RALLY-PAC

The Rally-Pac instrument cluster was a popular option on Mustang GTs. Mounted on the top side of the steering column, it featured a tachometer on the left and a clock on the right. The 6,000 rpm tachometer was used with all engines except the high-performance V-8, which had an 8,000 rpm tachometer. By 1966, the Rally-Pac was standard on GTs.

KEY FEATURES
1965 Mustang Fastback

- **Production:** 77,079 units

- **First year for fastback body style**

- **GT model debuts**

- **289 Hi-Po engine debuts**

- **Five new colors**

UNDER THE HOOD
All Mustang GTs were equipped with one of Ford's V-8 engines

IDENTIFICATION
All Mustangs had Ford block letters across the front edge of the hood

DRIVING LIGHTS FOR THE GT PACKAGE

One of the most distinguishing characteristics of the inaugural Mustang GT was its driving lights, located inside the front grille. These lights (often referred to as fog lamps) were common on race cars of the day and added extra illumination for road racing. The Mustang GT's driving lights were connected to the two horizontal chrome bars that emanated from the sides of the center emblem.

The lighting package was offered as an option on all Mustangs but was standard on all GT models. A switch on the left side of the dashboard activated the driving lights.

TURN SIGNALS
Amber signal lights were surrounded by a chrome bezel

A Natural for Drag Racing

IN 1965–66 THE MUSTANG achieved its earliest racing successes at the drag strip. Ford Motor Company was already dominating the drag circuit with bigger cars like the Fairlane-based Thunderbolt, so a lightweight car with a shorter wheelbase and weighing a thousand pounds less was a natural winner. Bob Tasca Ford of Providence, Rhode Island, which had long been known as a performance-car dealer, had successfully campaigned a big-block-engined Thunderbolt before adopting the Mustang. When Tasca took the same big-block engines and shoehorned them into Mustangs, the cars were highly successful in their class at National Hot Rod Association (NHRA) events around the country. Other famous race teams, including those of drag-racing legends Gas Rhonda and Les Ritchey, also dominated with Mustangs.

BILL LAWTON
Driver Bill Lawton drove this Mustang in the '65 season for Tasca Ford.

LES RITCHEY

Driver Les Ritchey stacked up wins in the Performance Associates–sponsored 1965 A/FX Mustang.

GAS RHONDA

Russ Davis Ford sponsored this factory experimental class drag car. Former dancing instructor Gas Rhonda piloted the team's racers for many seasons.

1966 TASCA FORD A/FX DRAG CAR

The Tasca Ford race team was one of the first to campaign Mustangs at the drag strip. Most of Tasca's cars were raced in the popular A/FX (factory experimental) class. Bill Lawton drove this car in the '66 NHRA season.

WEEKEND WARRIORS

Drag racing was the most popular auto sport in the United States during the 1960s. To boost participation at the grassroots level, the National Hot Rod Association offered several racing classes for cars that were essentially factory stock with only a few modifications. Entries in these classes were often "weekend warriors," people who drove their cars during the week and raced them on weekends.

Modifications often meant simply replacing the stock rear tires with a pair of drag slicks. The Mustang, with its excellent power-to-weight ratio, was a popular choice for weekend racing and fared well at tracks across the country.

A weekend warrior stages his '65 Mustang

1966 Mustang Convertible

1966 GRILLE ORNAMENT

FORD ADOPTED A "why mess with success?" attitude for the 1966 production model, making only minor changes to the Mustang. The now-famous galloping horse emblem and corral surround became free-floating on horizontal grille bars, creating a sleeker front view than in previous years. A slight variation to the scallop side trim and a restyled gas cap completed the exterior changes. On the interior, the instrument panel was redesigned with five round gauges: a large central speedometer, fuel gauge, oil pressure gauge, ammeter, and a coolant temperature gauge. Although the Mustang hardtop model outsold the convertible, the rag top was still a hot seller. More than 70,000 Mustang convertibles were sold in the 1966 model year. A base model convertible could be had for about $50 less than the price of the fastback, so it was an attractive buy. Perhaps that was why the convertible outsold the fastback nearly three to one.

NEW WHEELS
Stylish steel wheels were optional for 1966.

REFINED RAGTOP
Because of its classic, simplified design, many consider the 1966 Mustang the best car of the first three model years. Sporting a convertible top, it represents the quintessential freewheeling pony car.

WINDSHIELD
Upper windshield tint was optional

GRILLE EMBLEM
For the first time, the galloping horse and corral surround were free-floating

ANTENNA
For an additional $57.51 the buyer could order a radio

A LUXURY INTERIOR FOR TRUE MUSTANG FANS

One of the more desirable options Ford offered for 1965–66 Mustangs was the Pony Interior. Officially known as the Interior Decor Group Option, this package featured distinct upgrades over the standard cockpit, notably an embossed panel depicting galloping mustangs on the back supports of all four seats. The doors were accentuated with specially molded panels, pistol-grip handles, and courtesy lights. Walnut-grained vinyl appliqués brought a more upscale look to the dashboard, while other touches of chrome trim added flash. The optional console completed the package, giving the Mustang owner a true custom interior.

This 1966 convertible has the deluxe interior featuring (inset) the embossed pony seatbacks

CONVERTIBLE BOOT
In the down position, the top was covered with a vinyl snap-on boot color-keyed to the interior

NEW COLOR
Emberglo was a new color option for the 1966 model

MIRROR
An optional remote mirror was available as a part of a visiblity package for $29.81

ROCKER PANEL
New rocker panel trim was standard on all models except the GT

SIDE SCOOP
Scoop trim was slightly revised for the '66 model

KEY FEATURES

1966 Mustang Convertible

- **Production:** 72,119 units
- **New grille pattern**
- **New instrument cluster**
- **Embossed pony interior**
- **Three new colors, including Emberglo**

REDESIGNED FRONT GRILLE

Ford saw very little reason to make big changes in the Mustang for 1966, but a cosmetic upgrade here and there was in order. One of the more obvious revisions was a sleeker front grille. The somewhat unnoticeable honeycomb grille pattern on the 1964–65 models gave way to a chrome multibar pattern set behind the corral-encased galloping horse front emblem.

1966 Mustang Coupe

NEW GAS CAP FOR 1966

MANY COLLECTORS PREFER the 1966 model coupe, despite the high number that were produced. The refinements made that year, although subtle, gave the car a more classic look. The GT option continued with the some of the items in the package being available individually. The Hi-Po, or High Performance, engine option continued to be available for the 1966 model year. Any model could be ordered with the Hi-Po for added power and performance. When fitted out with a 289 Hi-Po engine, four-speed transmission, and limited-slip differential, the Mustang became a hot street machine. Added to that, a special handling package including stiffer front and rear springs, larger front and rear shock absorbers, 22:1 steering ratio, and a large-diameter front stabilizer bar transformed the Mustang into the ultimate road racer.

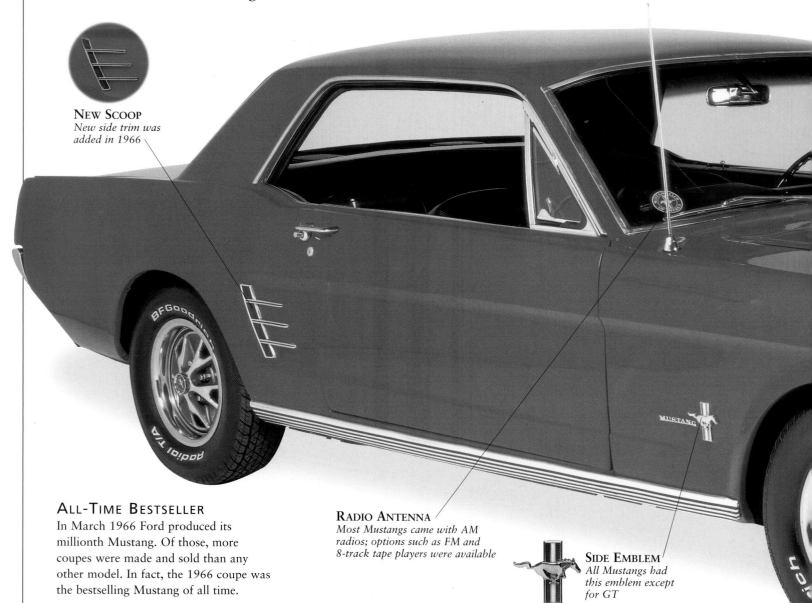

NEW SCOOP
New side trim was added in 1966

ALL-TIME BESTSELLER
In March 1966 Ford produced its millionth Mustang. Of those, more coupes were made and sold than any other model. In fact, the 1966 coupe was the bestselling Mustang of all time.

RADIO ANTENNA
Most Mustangs came with AM radios; options such as FM and 8-track tape players were available

SIDE EMBLEM
All Mustangs had this emblem except for GT

KEY FEATURES
1966 Mustang Coupe

- **Production:** 499,751 units
- Bright hood lip molding
- New styled steel wheels
- Revised side scoop trim
- New rocker panel molding

289 HI-PO ENGINE

Ford offered several engine options for the Mustang in 1965, but the true lovers of speed and muscle opted for a 289cid, V-8 Hi-Po powerplant. This engine, which came equipped with a 600 cfm Autolite four-barrel carburetor, delivered a neck-snapping 271 hp. It is easily identified by its chrome air cleaner and valve covers. "Hi-Po" was Ford's own nickname for "High Performance," and the name appears on the side emblems of all Mustangs that were endowed with the more powerful engine.

Mustangs with the Hi-Po engine are often called "K-cars" because their vehicle identification numbers (VIN) include the letter K

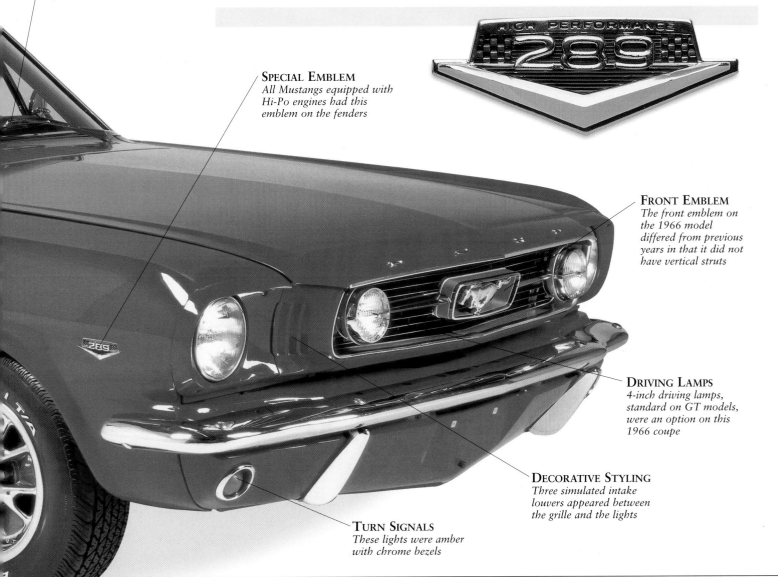

WINDSHIELD WIPERS
Wipers were controlled by an electric motor with a vacuum-operated washer system

SPECIAL EMBLEM
All Mustangs equipped with Hi-Po engines had this emblem on the fenders

FRONT EMBLEM
The front emblem on the 1966 model differed from previous years in that it did not have vertical struts

DRIVING LAMPS
4-inch driving lamps, standard on GT models, were an option on this 1966 coupe

DECORATIVE STYLING
Three simulated intake louvers appeared between the grille and the lights

TURN SIGNALS
These lights were amber with chrome bezels

1966 Mustang Fastback

THE LAST PRODUCTION YEAR for the original Mustang fastback was 1966. This would prove to be an excellent year for the coupe but fastback sales would drop nearly 50 percent. In its first two annual runs – from its introduction in April 1964 through the end of 1965 – Ford sold nearly 700,000 Mustangs. In 1966 Ford not only broke the 1 million sales mark with the Mustang, but also sold a record-setting 607,568 units. Because only a little more than 35,000 of these were fastbacks this model is highly collectible today. It was a banner year for the Mustang, but it was also the last year Ford would solely own the pony-car podium. General Motors was readying the Chevrolet Camaro and Pontiac Firebird for launch the following year. Chrysler and American Motors would follow with similar pony-car models. By the end of 1966, the stage was set for battles to come.

KEY FEATURES
1966 Mustang Fastback

- **Production:** 35,698 units
- **New gas cap on GT models**
- **Driving lamps standard on GT**
- **Most came with AM radio**
- **First year for standard backup lights**

A HOT ROD FASTBACK
This GT was loaded with high-performance options such as the 289 Hi-Po engine, close-ratio four-speed transmission, and the special handling package.

V-8 SIDE EMBLEM
A Mustang with a V-8 engine can be spotted right away by the side badge that indicates the type of powerplant

UNDER THE HOOD
All Mustang GTs were equipped with one of Ford's V-8 engines

LETTERS
GTs sported "Mustang" on the lower front fender, although this was deleted on the export T-5

T-5: A HORSE WITH NO NAME

An unusual version of the Mustang, dubbed the T-5 (the original product code designation for the Mustang program), was sold in Germany between 1964 and 1979. Part of Ford's marketing plan was to sell the pony car to both US military and German consumers. Trademark rights for the name "Mustang," however, were already taken by a truck and motorbike manufacturer. Ford was forced to delete all reference to the name on models exported to the German market.

The Mustang emblems on the side were replaced with T-5 badges and, in the case of this 1966 GT, a GT nameplate

This appears to be a Mustang GT, but look closely because it lacks the word "Mustang"

The center hub on the T-5 steering wheel sported the "pony-on-stripes" crest, but there was no mention of its Mustang roots. The speedometer read kilometers per hour instead of miles per hour as on the US Mustang

EXIT VENTS
The Mustang's Silent-Flo ventilation system improved air quality in the interior of fastback models

SIDE STRIPES
The GT racing stripes were a styling theme carried over from race cars of the day

CLEAN SIDE
For a cleaner look, the chrome rocker panels were not used on GT models

TRIMLESS
The chrome trim side scoop was not used on GT models

STYLISH WHEELS
New steel wheels added a more aggressive appearance over the standard hubcaps

1964½–1966 Memorabilia

THE FIRST OWNERS MANUAL

ONE MEASURE of the first Mustang's success was the number of commercial spinoffs the car generated. Kids could be seen riding on driveways in Mustang pedal cars, one of many marketing tools created to get parents through the doors of car dealerships. Small promotional models of the Mustang were also sold at Ford dealerships. For more serious scale-miniature lovers, Mustang model car kits could be painted and glued into small-scale displays to the builder's liking. Early Mustangs are still icons for the American sports car buff. Today, toy models of the original Mustang are readily available on the shelves of toy and department stores, and all vintage Mustang paraphernalia is highly collectible. Proud Mustang owners avidly collect dealer promotional items, including brochures and scale models. Original Mustang toys and model kits fetch handsome prices at toy shows and swap meets.

PEDAL CAR

This rare pedal car manufactured by the AMF Corporation depicting a 1964 Mustang is high on the collectibles list. Selling in dealerships for a paltry $12.95 when it was first distributed, an original fine or restored condition pedal car can command well over $500 today.

STICK SHIFT
Shift lever added realism

WINDSHIELD
This was molded in clear plastic

STEERING WHEEL
Three-spoke steering wheel emulated the real Mustang

SIDE EMBLEM
Decal emblem approximated its counterpart on the full-scale car

WHEEL COVERS
Hubcaps came replete with spinners

TAILLIGHTS
One-piece bezels had decal inserts

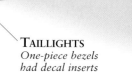

MODEL CAR KITS

Car modeling was one of the predominant hobbies among adolescents in the 1960s. Model manufacturing companies such as AMT, MPC, and Revell took advantage of the Mustang's popularity. Mustang kits can still be found on the shelves of hobby shops.

FRICTION CARS

These toys had friction motors that allowed them to run on their own power.

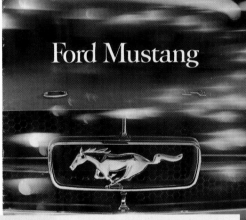

GRILLE
The pedal car featured a grille similar to the full-size car

BROCHURES

Dealer brochures are highly collectible among Mustang owners and fans. Original sales materials from the 1960s are more valuable than ever today, now that reproductions are available at a fraction of the cost.

BUMPERS
Silver paint imitated the chrome units on the full-size car

ADVERTISEMENTS

Ads for the original Mustang can be easy to find. This one from the June 1964 issue of *Motor Trend* depicts the enjoyment of driving a Mustang.

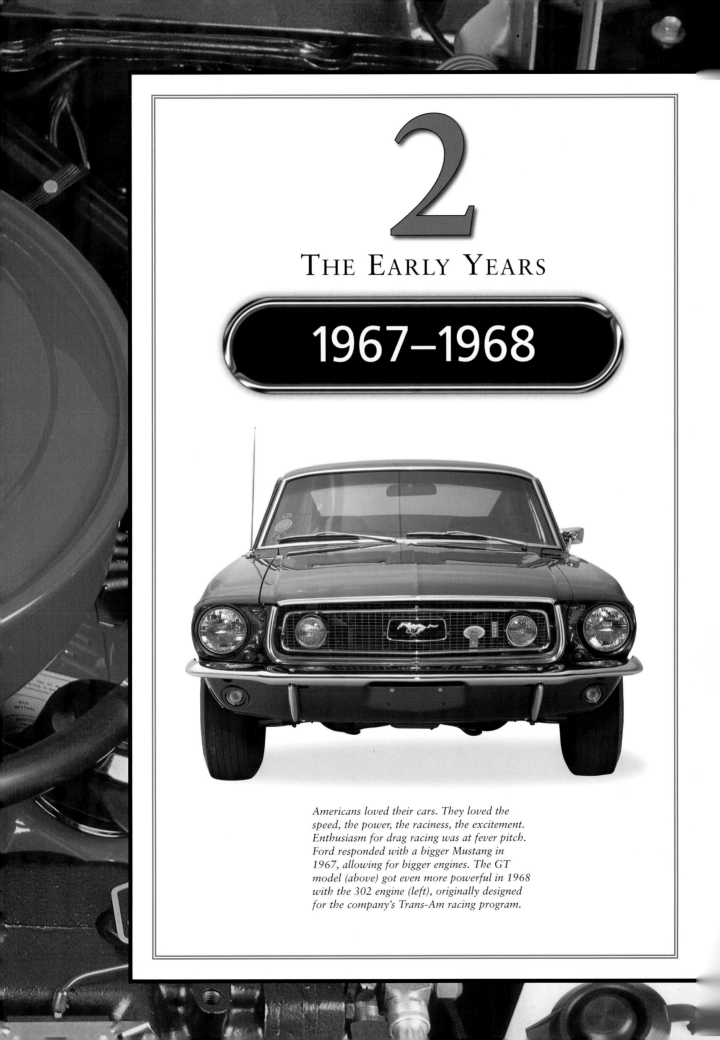

2

THE EARLY YEARS

1967–1968

Americans loved their cars. They loved the speed, the power, the raciness, the excitement. Enthusiasm for drag racing was at fever pitch. Ford responded with a bigger Mustang in 1967, allowing for bigger engines. The GT model (above) got even more powerful in 1968 with the 302 engine (left), originally designed for the company's Trans-Am racing program.

The Competition Heats Up

BY 1967 THE HONEYMOON WAS OVER in terms of Mustang's unquestioned domination of the pony car market. Chevrolet's Camaro, Pontiac's Firebird, and Plymouth's Barracuda were nipping at sales. Among Ford's immediate responses was a burst of marketing creativity. The company began looking for major regional markets that might be hungry for special-edition Mustangs. California accounted for a large portion of Ford's Mustang sales; 20 percent of all Mustangs were sold in the Los Angeles area alone. Thus was born the 1968 Mustang GT/CS, a limited edition commonly referred to as the "California Special." Production of the GT/CS production was restricted to fewer than 5,000 units available exclusively through the Southern California Dealers Group. The

CALIFORNIA SPECIAL
The rear decorative side scoops, blacked-out grille, and side striping were among the features of this special edition car. Mustang regional editions like this one sold out nationwide.

GT/CS package was sold as an option for hardtops only and included modifications such as an emblem-free, blacked-out grille with rectangular fog lamps; decorative side scoops; special side/rear striping; indigenous scripts; a built-in rear spoiler; and sequential taillights. Colorado Ford dealers offered a similar Mustang, dubbed the GT/HCS for "High Country Special."

Cars & Culture 1967–1968

1967: The Camaro	1967: Mustang Redesign	1967: Convertible
Performance quickly became the name of the game among pony-car market competitors. The 1967 launch of the Chevrolet Camaro, with its optional 396 engine, marked the beginning of the Mustang's serious race to hang onto its share of sales.	Mustang was completely redesigned for 1967. The car was now larger and sleeker; it also rode better thanks to an improved suspension system.	For the first time, this model year's convertible featured a two-pane tempered safety glass rear window that folded down with the roof.

'67 Chevrolet Camaro	*1967 Mustang fastback*	*1967 Mustang convertible*

People Behind the Mustang

BOB TASCA

The top performance-oriented Ford dealership, which was located in East Providence, Rhode Island, was Tasca Ford. In the late 1960s, owner Bob Tasca was instrumental in moving the Mustang up the performance ladder to meet and beat its competition. While the 390 was the most powerful Mustang engine available in 1967, the competition had that topped. Tasca noticed that as a result, Mustangs he sold were not holding their own on local streets and drag strips, and this was hurting sales at Tasca Ford.

The Mustang's racing power was something Tasca knew a lot about because, as a key player in Ford's high-profile presence on drag racing circuits, he maintained a Mustang race car and driver. Tasca had been among the first, in fact, to race Mustangs on the circuit. He and his

Bob Tasca with one of his Mustang drag cars

staff of automotive performance technicians decided to take the issue of Mustang engine power into their own hands. Using what they found in Ford's service parts catalog, Tasca's team created a powerful engine they dubbed the KR-8. It started with a 428 police-car block; added were 427 low-riser heads, a hotter cam, 10.7:1 pistons, free-flowing exhaust manifolds, a 735 CFM Holley carburetor, and a cast-iron intake. The following year, using the engine (renamed 428 Cobra Jet by Ford), Tasca's cars would blow away the drag-racing competition. In 1968, the Cobra Jet engine would be incorporated into the production Mustangs and would become a mainstay of the line. In addition to his success in the sales and racing arenas, Tasca would go on to spend a number of years as a quality consultant to Ford Motor Company worldwide.

1967-68: Racing	1968: 302 Engine	1968: Hot Wheels
Ford's racing program was going great guns in 1966 and '67. In both years, the contest for the Trans-Am racing title came down to the last race of the year. And in both years, driver Jerry Titus was called in to take the title for Ford.	Originally created to increase engine displacement in Ford's Trans-Am race cars, the 302 engine, rated at 230 hp, made its way into the Mustang production line in 1968. It would remain the base V-8 for the entire Ford line through 1973.	In 1968, Mattel would revolutionize the toy market with the introduction of the Hot Wheels line of miniature die-cast cars.

Jerry Titus behind the wheel

1968 302cid engine

1968 Hot Wheels Mustang

1967–1968 Concept

IT COULD EASILY BE SAID THAT the 1967 Mustang was designed from the inside out. Changes in the car at this time were all about improving power and performance. The style of the '67 exterior did not deviate much from the themes that had made the original such a hit; rather, it was as if the car had taken on pounds in all directions. While the wheelbase remained the same, at 108 inches, the newly designed body increased by 2 inches in length and more than 2.5 inches in width to accommodate a big-block engine. Ford took every possible opportunity to promote a high-performance image.

As part of its effort to connect its name with the ultimate performance machine, in 1967 Ford added the Mustang name to a streamlined front-engined dragster, the "Super Mustang." This concept exhibition racer was powered by a single overhead cam (known as SOHC) 427cid fuel-injected engine, the same powerplant used by the popular Ford drag racers of the day.

HORSE RACING
A clear cover on the nose of the Super Mustang is decorated with the famous galloping horse.

FORD SUPER MUSTANG
This concept dragster might not look like the production Mustangs of 1967, but it proudly wore the Mustang name. At a time when racy performance was everything, Ford created the Super Mustang to promote the power under the 1967 Mustang hood and its winning potential at dragstrips across the country.

BUBBLE-TOP
Clear canopy offered protection to the driver as well as providing an aerodynamic advantage

SLICK TIRES
To get the most traction possible, the Super Mustang used drag slicks

EXHAUST
Special tuned headers exited through a slot in the body

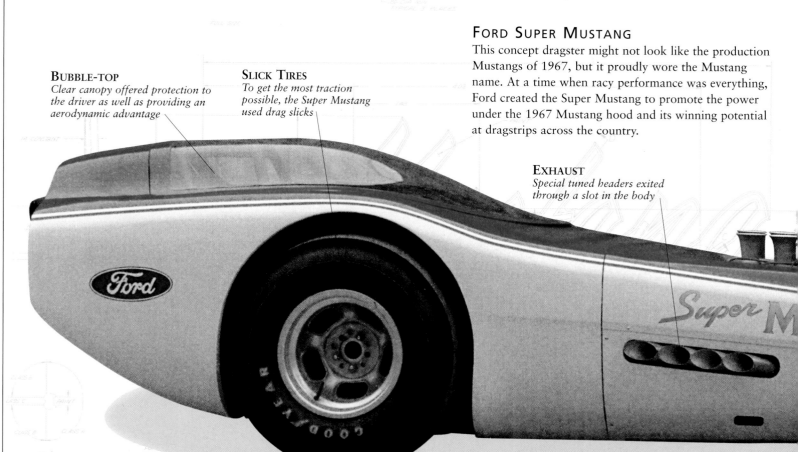

1967 CLAY MODELS

In Mustang's early days Ford designers worked out their ideas for new models in clay. Dozens of 1:1 scale clay models were constructed for the purpose of presenting styling options for any given model year to Ford management, who would make the final choices for production. Many clay models differed from side to side so alternate ideas could be quickly presented. Models were well finished with slick painted surfaces, rolling wheels, and sometimes even clear windows. Several of these clay Mustangs were created. When Ford was finished with them, they were destroyed. The models pictured here display some of the ways Ford toyed with styling on the 1967–68 model. The dates on the front-view photos indicate that these were all presented on the same day; note that various grille designs were interchanged on the same car. Clay models are still used in automobile design today, although the computer has partially replaced them as a design tool.

Grille bar proposals underwent careful scrutiny before a change was made

Designers presented widely varying side panels for the '67 model

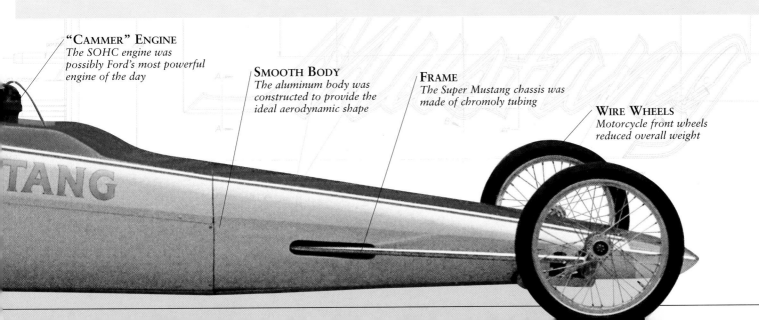

"CAMMER" ENGINE
The SOHC engine was possibly Ford's most powerful engine of the day

SMOOTH BODY
The aluminum body was constructed to provide the ideal aerodynamic shape

FRAME
The Super Mustang chassis was made of chromoly tubing

WIRE WHEELS
Motorcycle front wheels reduced overall weight

1967 Mustang Coupe

1967 GAS CAP

ALTHOUGH THE 1967 MUSTANG'S wheelbase remained at 108 inches, the car was otherwise completely redesigned for that year. In many ways the 1967 coupe appeared to be just a slightly larger version of the original, but more sophisticated styling gave the car an identity of its own. The front grille retained the galloping horse with its corral surround, but the enlarged opening gave the car a more natural look. The side scoops, though nonfunctional, were designed as two smaller scoops with inlets and painted the body color – quite different from the chrome tacked-on look of the scoops on 1966 models. All of these features contributed to a clean, polished look.

FANCY WHEELS
Highly stylized hubcaps were standard in 1967.

PLAIN VANILLA
Though it was not as flashy as a fastback or convertible, the coupe continued to outsell its counterparts. The car was redesigned for 1967 to hold bigger block engines.

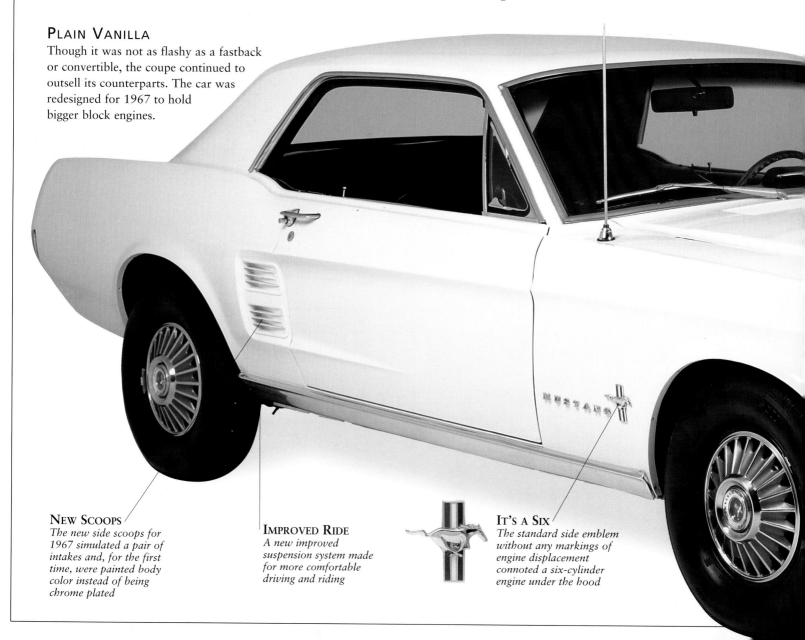

NEW SCOOPS
The new side scoops for 1967 simulated a pair of intakes and, for the first time, were painted body color instead of being chrome plated

IMPROVED RIDE
A new improved suspension system made for more comfortable driving and riding

IT'S A SIX
The standard side emblem without any markings of engine displacement connoted a six-cylinder engine under the hood

SPECIFICATIONS

MODEL Shown	1967 Mustang Coupe
PRODUCTION	325,853 units
BODY STYLES 1967–68	Convertible, coupe, fastback
CONSTRUCTION	Unibody chassis/body
ENGINES	200cid I-6 (1967–68) 289cid V-8 (1967–68) 302cid V-8 (1968) 390cid V-8 (1967–68) 427cid V-8 (1968) 428cid V-8 Cobra Jet (1968)
POWER OUTPUT	120 hp (200cid I-6) to 390 hp (427cid V-8)
TRANSMISSION	Three- and four-speed manual or three-speed automatic
SUSPENSION	Independent front with coil springs and wishbones; semielliptic leaf springs at rear
BRAKES	Drums standard, discs optional on front
MAXIMUM SPEED	115 mph (185 km/h) (390cid) 0–60 mph (0–96 km/h) 7.4 seconds (390cid) 0–100 mph (0–161 km/h) 15.6 seconds (390cid) A.F.C. 12 mpg (320 hp V-8)

BREAD-AND-BUTTER SIX-CYLINDER MUSTANGS

Ford offered low-budget, straight-six-cylinder Mustangs from the start, and these more affordable editions enabled the company to sell the car in high volume. Approximately 30 percent of Mustangs sold in the first five years were powered by six cylinders. Ford even got behind the six-cylinder engine in ad campaigns and released special upscale "Sprint" versions of the car for several years. The basic six was available with a one-barrel carburetor and was offered with three-speed, four-speed, or automatic transmission.

The 200cid, six-cylinder engine powered base-level Mustangs

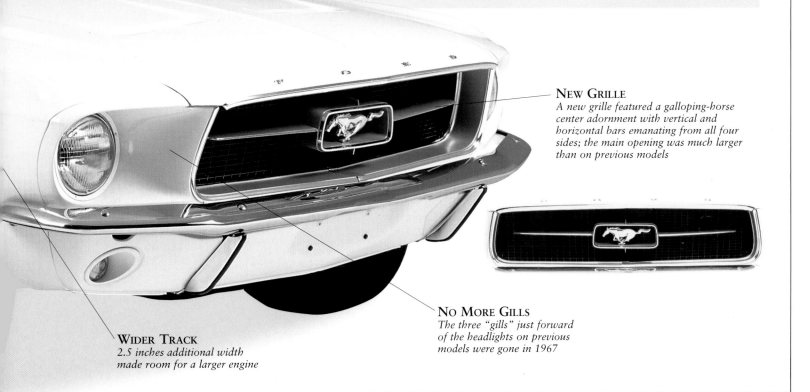

NEW GRILLE
A new grille featured a galloping-horse center adornment with vertical and horizontal bars emanating from all four sides; the main opening was much larger than on previous models

NO MORE GILLS
The three "gills" just forward of the headlights on previous models were gone in 1967

WIDER TRACK
2.5 inches additional width made room for a larger engine

1967 Mustang Variations

IN 1967 THE COMPETION WAS BEGINNING to enjoy a respectable share of the pony car market. Eating into Mustang sales figures were the Chevrolet Camaro (220,906), Mercury Cougar (150,983), Pontiac Firebird (82,560), and Plymouth Barracuda (62,534). Still, Mustang managed to outsell its nearest competitor, the Chevrolet Camaro, by a ratio of two to one. As in previous years, the car-buying public could choose from the coupe, convertible, and 2+2 fastback. The lack of chrome side trim on 1967 models made for a more subdued appearance than in previous years. The fastback, however, took on a much heftier look due to its extended roof. Ford reported sales of 71,042 fastback Mustangs, 44,808 convertibles, and 356,271 coupes that year.

KEY FEATURES
1967 MUSTANG GT FASTBACK

- **Production:** 71,042 units
- **Extended roof**
- **29 colors available**
- **Fog lamps available**
- **Ribbed rear panel available**

EXTENDED ROOF
For the first time the roof was extended all the way to the rear of the car

STRIPES
The 1967 GT package included standard rocker panel stripes

GT FASTBACK
The 2+2 fastback is shown here in GT attire. As in previous years, driving lamps, side stripes, and dual exhausts were all part of the 1967 GT package.

HOOD RECESSES
A hood with dual recesses was optional on 1967 models

1967 Mustang Convertible

This was the first year the convertible featured a two-pane glass rear window that folded down with the roof. It was also the last year of the 289 Hi-Po. Only 472 cars were equipped with that engine, making them extremely rare today.

Top Cover
The convertible's top was covered by a boot that matched the interior of the car; tops were available in black or white

Wheels
These styled steel wheels would see their last year on 1967 Mustangs

Custom Rear
The fastback could be ordered with a ribbed rear panel replacing the chrome bezels.

Block Letters
"F-O-R-D" would not be seen across the front edge of the hood again until 1974

Lamps Return
Driving lights were similar to those found on earlier GT models

Front Bumper
The bumper styling was similar to the previous models with standard lower bumperettes

390 Engine, the Mustang's First Big Block

To meet the increasing performance demands of the marketplace, Ford added the Thunderbird's 390cid, 320 hp big-block engine to the Mustang. The 1967 redesign had in fact been worked largely to accommodate this larger engine. The 390 used cast-iron intake and exhaust manifolds and a single 600 cfm Holley four-barrel carburetor. Mustangs with 390s had dual exhaust systems. The era of big-block performance had begun; 28,800 Mustangs were equipped with 390s in 1967.

The 390 put the 1967 Mustang in the performance race

1968 Mustang GT

1968 POP-OPEN
GT GAS CAP

The GT package remained the top choice for performance-oriented Mustang buyers in 1968. The previous year's increase in body dimensions allowed Ford to introduce its new, larger 427cid and 428cid engines. These engines, combined with the GT's standard front disc brakes, performance tires, heavy-duty suspension, and dual exhausts with chrome quad outlets, elevated this pony car to its raciest version yet. New cosmetics also were included for 1968, with new styled steel wheels in chrome or painted silver with special GT hub caps, and new "C" stripe that accented the side scoop. Also available was a competition handling package that included larger 15-inch wheels, firmer suspension, and a limited rear slip axle.

KEY FEATURES

1968 MUSTANG GT FASTBACK

- **Production:** 61,980 units
- **302 and 428 engines introduced**
- **New GT emblem and hubcaps**
- **New striping**
- **Power front disc brakes standard**

1968 MUSTANG GT FASTBACK

The Mustang GT could be considered the top-of-the-line Mustang for that model year. In addition to more power and performance features, the GT, like all 1968 Mustangs, could be equipped with an array of stylish options, including an overhead console, horizontal rear bar grille panel, styled steel wheels, driving lamps, and a pop-open gas cap.

ROOF VENTS
The fastback roof got more louvers for fresh-air venting

SPORTSROOF
The fastback, branded by Ford as a "SportsRoof," trailed fully to the rear body panel on the revised Mustang

SMALL TRUNK
As in previous years, fastbacks had limited trunk space compared to coupes

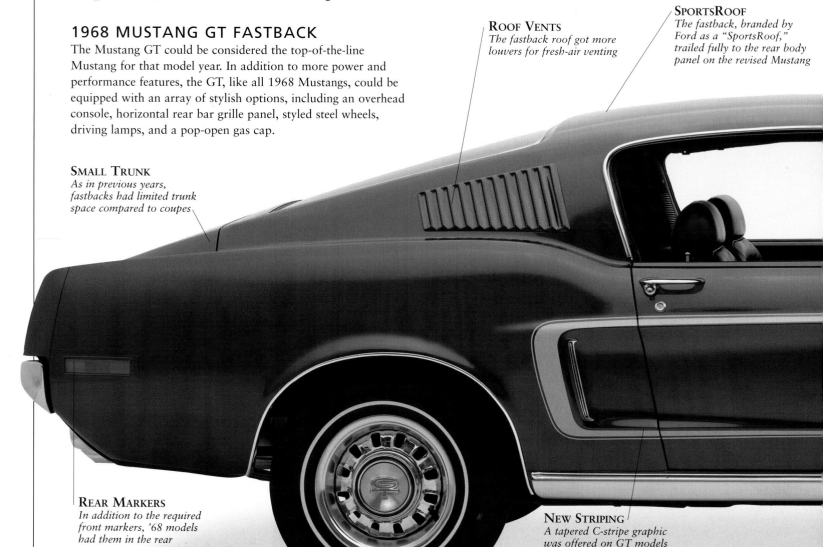

REAR MARKERS
In addition to the required front markers, '68 models had them in the rear

NEW STRIPING
A tapered C-stripe graphic was offered on GT models for the first time in 1968

RARE DELUXE BENCH SEAT INTERIOR

The 1968 Mustang fastback pictured below is one of only 256 fastback models Ford delivered with the deluxe bench seat option installed in that model year. Although the seatbacks featured bucket-seat styling and at first glance the entire seating installation appears to have a bucket design, the bottom seat cushion was all one unit. Another attractive feature of this bench seat was the folding center armrest, a novelty, actually considered a luxury, at that time. The Deluxe Interior Option included extra chrome trim on the door panels and ornaments on the seatbacks. The entire seating unit moved forward and backward on a pair of rails. Bench seats were offered on the Mustang from its inception through 1970, when they were dropped altogether in favor of the sportier-looking high-back bucket seats, which sold better than the bench option. The Mustang featured here is one of only ten existing Mustang GT fastback models with the bench seat option that have been deemed restorable.

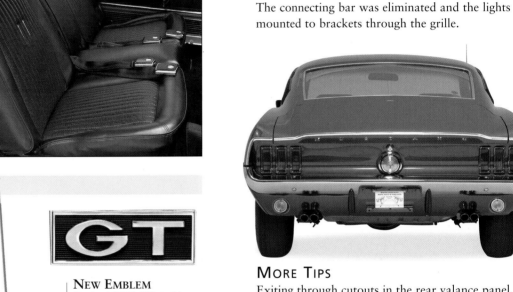

A NEW LOOK
The 1968 GT received revised running lights. The connecting bar was eliminated and the lights mounted to brackets through the grille.

MORE TIPS
Exiting through cutouts in the rear valance panel, quad exhaust tips gave the GT a look of power.

WINDSHIELD BAND
Tinted banding on the windshield was available as an option

GT

NEW EMBLEM
Revised 1968 GT emblem was mounted higher on the front fender than on previous year's models

GT HUBCAPS
All 1968 GT models came with these attractive steel wheels with "GT" center caps

SIDE MARKERS
Federal regulations required all 1968 models to have front end markers

1968 Mustang Variations

1968 GAS CAP

IN 1968 THE FORD MUSTANG was in its second year of restyling, so there were only minor cosmetic changes to the exterior of the hardtop, convertible, and fastback models. Ford simplified the front-grille fascia by removing the horizontal bars on either side of the main emblem and adding a single line of trim around its outer edges. The corral surrounding the galloping horse was reduced in thickness proportional to the outer trim ring. The twin side scoops were replaced with a simple one-piece chrome unit, and for the first time, script-style lettering was used instead of block letters on the side trim. Federally mandated shoulder belts also appeared for the first time.

TOP SELLER
Despite increased competition, the Mustang coupe continued to be the hottest selling pony car. Hardtop sales were just shy of a quarter-million for the 1968 model year.

BRIGHT IDEA
Ford has a better idea: turn signal indicators positioned in the hood recesses

SIZZLING PAINT
Candyapple Red was the hottest color in the Mustang line for 1968

NO DESIGNATION
For the first time in the car's history, the letters F-O-R-D do not appear on the lead edge of the hood

GT OR NOT GT?
At first glance this red 1968 convertible, with its fog lamps, C-stripe graphics, and flashy steel wheels, appears to be a Mustang GT. However, in the 1960s it was common to custom-order your car with just the options you wanted and no more. The original owners of this Mustang specified several GT options when purchasing their car, foregoing the full package. Two clues that this car is not a GT are its lack of a GT badge on the front fender and GT markings on the center hubs of the styled steel wheels.

FRONT SIDE MARKERS
Federal regulations stipulated side lights on front fenders

GOODBYE 289, HELLO 302

Ford engineers created the 302 to give the Mustang more engine displacement in their Trans-Am race cars, in which a maximum of 305cid, 5.0L was allowed. Thus a new engine for the Ford Mustang was born. The standard 302 was rated at 230 hp, 35 more than the 289. Transmission options remained the same for the 289, with three- and four-speed manuals and an automatic offered. A hopped-up 250 hp version of the 302 saw duty in the Shelby GT-350, but federal emission standards kept the engine from reaching its full potential. The 302 remained the base V-8 engine in the Ford line through 1973.

The 302 engine would be a powerhouse for years to come

KEY FEATURES
1968 MUSTANG CONVERTIBLE

- **Production:** 25,376 units
- 16 colors available
- 289 engine replaced by 302
- Chrome trim returns to scoop
- Seat belts and side markers

BEHIND THE WHEEL
The 1968 Mustang featured an energy-absorbing steering column and new two-spoke steering wheel.

SUSPENDED MIRROR
A first in 1968, the rearview mirror was mounted directly to the windshield glass instead of the frame

SCRIPTED STYLE
Script lettering replaced block letters

CHROME SCOOP
Chrome trim returns to the Mustang's side scoop after a year's absence

1967–1968 Drag Racing

THE 1968 FORD MUSTANG FOUND ITS HIGHEST level of racing success at the drag strip. The 428 Cobra Jet motor was embraced by racing teams running Ford products and proved to be more than up to the task in the hotly contested SS/E and SS/F classes.

The 428CJ was unleashed at the 1968 National Hot Rod Association (NHRA) Winternationals February 2–4 at Pomona Raceway in Pomona, California – one of drag racing's premier events. Ford was directly involved in sponsoring teams at the time and ended up with two of the country's top drivers, Hubert Platt and Al Joniec, in the finals of the SS/E race. Joniec got out of the gate faster and took the crown, but Platt set a new record and gave Ford a double win. Platt was legendary for his "Georgia Shaker" drag cars, a name that struck fear into anyone who had the misfortune of lining up against one of the driver's Ford factory-sponsored beasts. Platt rarely lost a race and was one of the first drivers to campaign stretched-nosed cars, which would later be termed "funny cars."

SUPER STOCK KING

Hubert Platt poses behind one of his legendary "Georgia Shaker" Super Stock cars. He drove this 1968 Mustang for the Foulger Ford team. Ford policy was to put its full corporate support behind such cars and drivers, to promote its performance image.

THE 428 COBRA JET DEBUTS

In 1967 Bob Tasca of Tasca Ford in East Providence, RI, had his service department beef up the engine power of his Mustang race car. Tasca's team put together a 428 police-car short block and aluminum intake manifold, 427 low-riser cylinder heads, special camshaft, 427 exhaust manifolds, and fuel system and suspension tweaks. It worked; the car was at least a full second quicker than its production brethren. Ford Chairman Henry Ford II liked this development, and thus was born the 428 Cobra Jet engine, unveiled at the 1968 National Hot Rod Association Winternationals drag meet at Pomona, California, where the Ford "factory" cars dominated the SS/E class and Al Joniec's Mustang became the eventual winner. The version that Ford engineers unleashed for production in 1968 featured a 735 cfm Holley carburetor, fed through an open element air cleaner sealed to the hood scoop opening by a large rubber gasket. The option required the GT Equipment Group, and either a four-speed manual or a C-6 Cruise-O-Matic transmission. The Cobra Jet engine option was offered in production cars through 1970 and would become a mainstay of the Shelby line.

This photo of the 428CJ was taken trackside at the Pomona Raceway during the 1968 Winternationals

FUNNY CAR

These doorless, fiberglass, stretch-nosed Mustangs pioneered the modern-day funny car. The term evolved out of the car's official designation as AA/FC, which signified a supercharged, nitro-burning "fuel coupe." Because of the car's unusual appearance, in the popular lexicon the FC soon was said to stand for "funny car."

"OHIO" GEORGE

Known for his Ford-powered 1933 Willys AA/FX, George Montgomery campaigned a Mustang for the 1967–68 NHRA season at the request of Ford management.

1967–1968 Trans-Am Racing

IN 1966 THE TRANS-AMERICAN Sedan Championship (Trans-Am) had reached the status of a professional road racing series with manufacturer support and winning drivers eager to participate in the event. In the last race that year, with the championship in the balance, Jerry Titus, editor of *Sports Car Graphic* magazine and driver of Shelby's GT350 B-Production, was called in at the last minute to win the title for Ford – which he did. By 1967 the Mustang team had stiffer competition from a factory-sponsored Mercury Cougar team prepared by Bill Stroppe of Pan American Lincoln race car fame, featuring drivers Dan Gurney and Parnelli Jones (who with George Follmer would win the Manufacturers' Cup in 1970). Again the final showdown came at the last race of the season in Kent, Washington. Titus and teammate Ronnie Bucknum won the race and the trophy, with Titus' Mustang winning the pole, setting the race record, and leading all but a few laps. Bucknum took second, and Mustang edged out Cougar for the championship by a scant two points for the year, 64 to 62.

TRANS-AM CHAMP
Driver Jerry Titus in Victory Lane after his win at Sebring in 1967.

1967 TRANS-AM MUSTANG
Driven by Jerry Titus's teammate, Ron Bucknum, this Mustang was one of the cars that helped Ford win the Trans-Am championship in 1967. Although this car's decals do not reflect it, Titus and Bucknum often raced their Mustangs under the crest of driver/designer Carroll Shelby's Terlingua Racing Team. Terlingua was a ghost town located on Shelby's Chiricahua ranch in Texas.

ROAD TO VICTORY

In 1967 the Ford Mustang had its second championship year in a row in SCCA Trans-Am road racing with a Mustang specially prepared by Shelby American with driver Jerry Titus at the wheel. Titus would die three years later in a crash at Road America, Wisconsin.

1968 TRANS-AM MUSTANG

The Titus/Bucknum crew changes tires en route to a fourth-place overall finish at the 24 Hours of Daytona in 1968.

1967–1968 Memorabilia

COLLECTORS WHO FAVOR THE 1967–68 MUSTANG find themselves in luck. The styling period may have been short, but the reproductions are numerous as well as popular. In fact, toy and kit manufacturing companies have produced so many miniature reproductions of the second-generation Mustang body styles that they are nearly as attainable as reproductions of the first body style. Die-cast and plastic reproductions, in both pre-built and kit forms, can be found in a wide range of scales. A number of dealer promotional models were circulated during those years as well, adding even more choices to the list. And like fans of any other styling year, 1967–68 enthusiasts must own a dealer brochure and owner's manual, plus print articles and advertisements from the day.

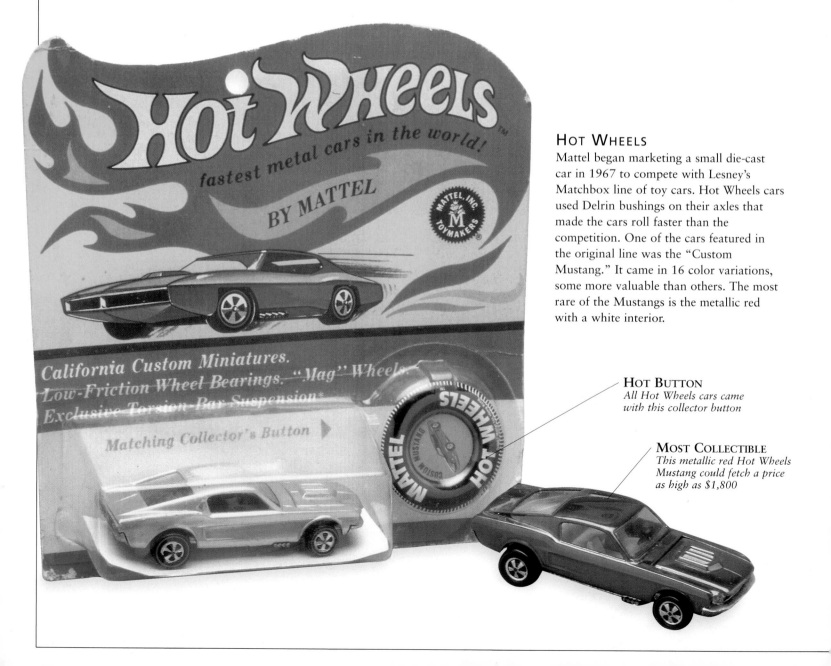

HOT WHEELS

Mattel began marketing a small die-cast car in 1967 to compete with Lesney's Matchbox line of toy cars. Hot Wheels cars used Delrin bushings on their axles that made the cars roll faster than the competition. One of the cars featured in the original line was the "Custom Mustang." It came in 16 color variations, some more valuable than others. The most rare of the Mustangs is the metallic red with a white interior.

HOT BUTTON
All Hot Wheels cars came with this collector button

MOST COLLECTIBLE
This metallic red Hot Wheels Mustang could fetch a price as high as $1,800

DEALER PROMOTION
This 1:12 scale miniature was marketed by Ford dealerships. It was manufactured by AMF, the same company that made the pedal car featured on page 36.

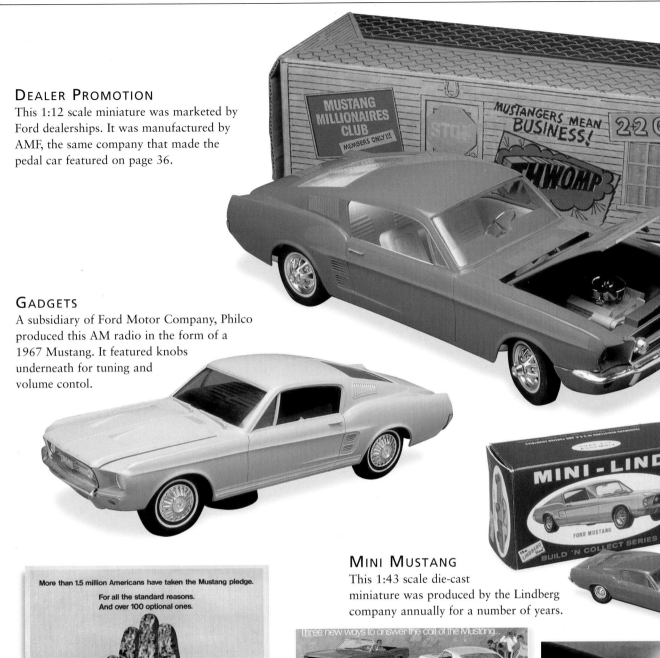

GADGETS
A subsidiary of Ford Motor Company, Philco produced this AM radio in the form of a 1967 Mustang. It featured knobs underneath for tuning and volume contol.

MINI MUSTANG
This 1:43 scale die-cast miniature was produced by the Lindberg company annually for a number of years.

More than 1.5 million Americans have taken the Mustang pledge.

For all the standard reasons.
And over 100 optional ones.

The standard reasons include items like floor-mounted stick shift and wall-to-wall carpeting. Items you'd have to pay extra for in many other cars. And with all this, Mustang is still America's lowest priced sports car with bucket seats!

How about Mustang options? Well, there are more than 100 offered so that you can personalize your Mustang.

You can get Stereo tape, air-conditioning, center console, Tilt-Away steering wheel, V-8's up to 390 cubic inches, and SelectShift, the automatic that also works like a manual. To name just a few. And they're all available on any Mustang—fastback, convertible, or hardtop. Why not see your Ford Dealer? He's the expert on Mustang—the car designed to be designed by you.

MUSTANG Ford

ADS
1967 ads such as this one often described the number of options that allowed the buyer to have a unique Mustang fitted to his personality.

BROCHURES
1967–68 dealer's brochures and owner's manuals are a must-have for the Mustang owner.

3

THE THOROUGHBRED YEARS

1969–1970

Ford Mustang reached a kind of golden maturity during 1969 and 1970, producing models such as the Boss and Mach I. Still, sales slowed as the competition from imitators increased. As a result, a Mustang staple, the GT (above and left), would fade away, only to return more than a decade later.

Power Is King

THE YEAR 1969 COULD BE CALLED THE PEAK of the musclecar era. That year, Detroit produced some of the most radical cars in automotive history. Gasoline was cheap, and high-compression big-block engines were guzzling it by the tankful. It was all about who was fastest in the quarter-mile, or who could run quickest between stoplights on Woodward Avenue (the hottest street-racing spot in Detroit). And if your car was not fast it had better at least look fast or you were nobody. Ford had been leading the race with its 1968 Cobra Jet Mustangs, but the other auto manufacturers were catching up. Names such as The Judge, Hemi 'Cuda, and Z-28 began to strike fear into Mustang owners who wanted their cars to rule the streets. Ford answered the call with models such as the Mach I and the Boss. Perhaps the stoutest Mustang of all, the Boss 429 was designed and named to intimidate. In 1970, the musclecar era would continue with many of these cars being refined and tuned to maximum performance.

BOSS OF THE STREET
The Boss 429 engine was Ford's powerful weapon against the Chrysler 426 Hemi at the height of the musclecar wars.

Cars & Culture 1969–1970

1969: Trans Am	1969: Mach I	1969: Boss 302
Pontiac had remained in the musclecar race with its own pony car, the Firebird, since 1967. Born in 1969 and named after the racing series was the Pontiac Trans Am, a slightly more upscale Firebird. Along with Chevrolet's Camaro, it would be Mustang's main competition for the next 30 years.	To stay in the musclecar game, Ford introduced the Mach I model in 1969. Resembling a fastback GT with fancier styling options and available with a 428cid big-block engine, the Mach I gave Mustang fastback sales a needed boost.	In 1969 a legend was born with the production of the first Ford Mustang Boss cars. Developed to secure approval for the company's revised 302 engine in Trans-Am racing, only 1,628 of these road-course winners were produced that first year.

1969 Pontiac Trans Am	*1969 Mustang Mach I*	*Mustang Boss 302*

People Behind the Mustang

ROBERT T. NEGSTAD

Robert (Bob) Negstad, during his three-decade career with Ford Motor Company, was associated with the Mustang program from the car's beginning. Negstad, senior engineer of the Mustang Development Department, was a chassis specialist who played a major role in the Mustang I design. His innovations included moving the FWD power unit to the rear of the car, necessitating placement of the engine midships, a revolutionary design for the time. Negstad's development group was responsible for Ford's earliest experiments with computer-aided suspension design technology. Ford adopted these computer programs and applied them as a basic working tool across all car lines.

In 1970, Negstad returned to Dearborn from England, where he had been part of a team working on Henry Ford II's GT40 racing program. Kar Kraft, a prototype shop in suburban Detroit, had produced the GT40s that Negstad had developed.

Bob Negstad with the Mustang I

The shop was selected to help produce the Boss 429 Mustangs, enabling Ford to use these monster engines on the NASCAR circuit. Kar Kraft's role was to support the Dearborn plant's assembly by installing the Boss 429 engines. These engines were so large that Kar Kraft had to modify the Mustang's front suspension assembly to squeeze them into the already large engine compartment.

Throughout his long career at Ford, Bob Negstad never stopped thinking of a better idea. During the development of the Mustang II, which would debut in 1974, this genius of the chassis set a new standard for smooth riding with his revolutionary "toilet seat" Mustang design: a U-shaped, isolated subframe on which the front suspension and engine were mounted. In the 1980s, he was the brains behind the SVO chassis.

Although Negstad died in early 2001, his love for and contributions to the Mustang will continue his legacy.

1969: Boss 429	1970: Trans-Am Cup	1970: Ghia Purchase
The Boss legend continued with the introduction of the Boss 429. Its 429 hemi-head V-8 engine was so big that it had to be retrofitted into the cars after they came off the Dearborn assembly line.	With Chevrolet and AMC as its archrivals, Ford went into the 1970 Trans-Am series backing team owner Bud Moore and drivers Parnelli Jones and George Follmer. Mustang won the Manufacturers' Cup with 72 points to the Javelin's 59 and Camaro's 40.	In 1970 Ford acquired the majority interest in the Italian design firm and coachbuilder, Ghia and Vignale. Ghia would become a subsidiary of Ford, commissioned to develop European styling for Ford automobiles, including the Mustang.

Boss 429 engine installation

Trans-Am racing

Ghia logo

1969–1970 Concept

FORESHADOWING THE RESTYLED 1969 Mustang, Ford began development of the Mach I show car in late 1966. The concept featured a lowered fastback roof with a kicked-up rear tail or "spoiler," and side scoops derived from the Ford GT-40 race car. Many of the show car's design features were incorporated into the 1969 production Mustang, and the Mach I name found its way onto an all-new model. Two significant events in 1968 also had an impact on the upcoming Mustang model year. In February, Henry Ford II surprised the automotive world by luring Semon E. "Bunkie" Knudsen away from General Motors to become the new Ford president. Knudsen hired one of Chevrolet's most talented designers, Larry Shinoda, to create eye-catching, high-performance Mustangs. Although these two men entered the picture late in the developmental process, both executed profound refinements to the 1969 production model. Knudsen's input dictated the Mustang's race-car feel, and Shinoda's influence added a combination of performance and style to the car.

MACH I SHOW CAR
Although the car was designed as far back as 1966, the Mach I styling features were readily recognizable on the 1969 Mustang.

HOOD PINS
A styling element derived from race cars

CLEAR COVERS
Clear plastic headlamp covers added a sporty look

LONG NOSE
The extreme forward-thrusting nose did not make the production model but foreshadowed future aerodynamic styling

GRILLE
The front grille featured a unique louvered panel

ROOFLINE
The most noted feature of the Mach I show car, its roofline, would heavily influence the production vehicle

QUAD EXHAUSTS
Four chrome exhaust tips exited below the rear bumper of the show car

GAS CAP
The show car had a roof-mounted gas cap similar to race cars of the day

BADGE
The pony-and-stripes badge was placed on the rear fender

FASTBACK FORESHADOWING
The rear of the Mach I had a spoilerlike design (common on road racers of the day) that was the most distinctive carryover onto the 1969 fastback model.

MUSTANG CLAY FRONT
Clay models were being used in 1969 to experiment with styling ideas. This one, for the 1969 production car, featured a much larger grille and larger side scoop.

SIDE SCOOP
The scoop on the production Mach I would be moved to the top of the rear fender

VENTILATION
A window within a window opened to provide fresh air

RACING MIRRORS
Teardrop-shaped race-style side mirrors were attached directly to the windows

MUSTANG CLAY REAR
Not all clay-model features made it onto the production car. The high spoiler-mounted taillights on this one were not included on the actual car, but the fastback styling and slab sides were.

1969 Mustang Convertible

1969 MUSTANG GT GAS CAP

BY 1969 THE MUSTANG had matured into the ultimate American sporting car. Gone were the pronounced side scallops; dual headlamps were introduced, with the extra pair of lights set into the outer area of the grille. Even the corralled horse was removed from the center of the grille and replaced by the pony-over-stripes emblem, set off-center to the driver's side. The same three body styles remained: coupe, convertible, and fastback. The 1969 Mustang retained the 108-inch wheelbase, but the overall length increased by almost 4 inches, and the girth expanded by almost half an inch. The Mustang GT line continued for 1969, joined by the new Mach I, Boss, and Grandé. All of these models took their toll on GT sales; they were continued in 1970, but the GT was not.

HORN
Ford offered a "Rim Blow" steering wheel option that allowed the driver to sound the horn by simply squeezing the wheel rim.

CLEAN LOOK
Side-vent windows were eliminated in 1969, making for a cleaner look and reduced wind noise

1969 GT STYLE
After this model year, the GT Equipment Group was discontinued until the early 1980s. With the four larger engines it included dual exhausts with quad outlets.

HOOD SCOOP
The GT Equipment Group option included an attractive but nonfunctional air scoop

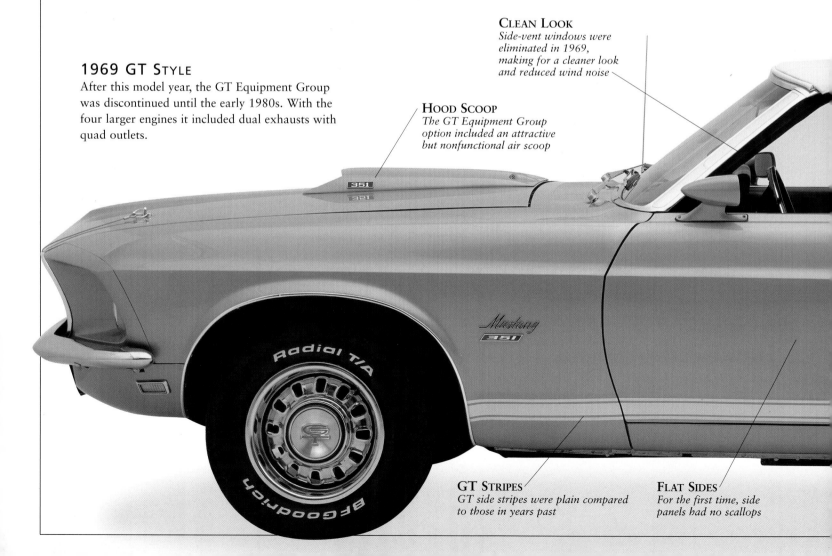

GT STRIPES
GT side stripes were plain compared to those in years past

FLAT SIDES
For the first time, side panels had no scallops

THE 351: A TALE OF TWO ENGINES

Two 351cid engines were available in the 1969 Mustang. These engines were built at Ford's Windsor, Ontario, plant, and both were known as the Windsor, or the 351W. The Windsor, which was a longer-stroke version of the basic 302 engine, was available as a two-barrel (250 hp) or a four-barrel (290 hp). The Windsor-based V-8 became the standard 5.0L engine until 1996.

The Windsor engine was Ford's 351cid powerplant in 1969

SPECIFICATIONS

MODEL SHOWN	1969 Mustang GT Convertible
PRODUCTION	14,746 units
BODY STYLES 1969–70	Convertible, coupe, fastback
CONSTRUCTION	Unibody chassis/body
ENGINES	200cid I-6 (1969–70) 250cid I-6 (1969–70) 302cid V-8 Boss (1969–70) 302cid V-8 (1969–70) 351cid V-8 (1969–70) 390cid V-8 (1969) 428cid V-8 Cobra Jet (1969–70) 429cid V-8 Boss (1969–70)
POWER OUTPUT	120 hp (200cid I-6) to 375 hp (429cid V-8 Boss)
TRANSMISSION	Three- and four-speed manual or three-speed automatic
SUSPENSION	Independent front with coil springs and wishbones; semielliptic leaf springs at rear
BRAKES	Drums standard; discs optional on front
MAXIMUM SPEED	121 mph (428cid, 335 hp V-8) 0–60 mph (0–96 km/h) 5.5 seconds (429cid V-8 Boss) 0–100 mph (0–161 km/h) 12.8 seconds (429cid V-8 Boss) A.F.C. 12 mpg (428cid V-8)

HEADLIGHTS
1969 models featured four sealed-beam headlights instead of two. This negated the need for fog lights on the GT model.

REAR VIEW
Both the 1969 convertible and coupe got a restyled rear end with a more rectangular taillight panel.

CONVERTIBLE TOP
Five-ply vinyl top folded down by hand

LUGGAGE RACK
Continued as an option in 1969

NEW TRIM
Resembling a reversed exhaust outlet, the trim mounted in place of a scoop received mixed reviews

STYLED WHEELS
Slotted steel wheels, standard on Mustang GT, were an option on other models

1969 Mustang Mach I

MACH I POP-OPEN
GAS CAP

TO ENHANCE ITS PERFORMANCE IMAGE and hang on to market share, Ford announced several new models for 1969. The Mach I was geared toward the performance crowd. The V-8 engine options were proof that muscle was everything in 1969. The 200cid I-6 was carried over in the new model year, as were the 302cid and 390cid V-8s. New for 1969 was the 351cid V-8, a small-block engine with 250 hp standard and a 290 hp version available. For pure power there was the 428cid big-block with two options: the 335 hp Cobra Jet V-8 with or without Ram-Air. More than 80 percent of all 1969 Mustangs sold were equipped with V-8 engines. Still, Mustang sales slipped as competition increased. A total of 299,824 units were sold, some 17,000 fewer than in 1968. The Mach I gave fastback models a nice sales boost.

> **KEY FEATURES**
> **1969 MUSTANG MACH I**
>
> • **Production:** 72,458 units
> • **First year for this model**
> • **Blacked-out hood treatment**
> • **Reflective body side tape stripes**
> • **High-back bucket seats**

THE PRODUCTION MACH I

The Mach I moniker derived from the original show car released by Ford in 1966. The Mach I was essentially a fastback GT with different stripes and a more upscale interior. With optional spoiler and window louvers, it was a car that did not escape notice on a Saturday night.

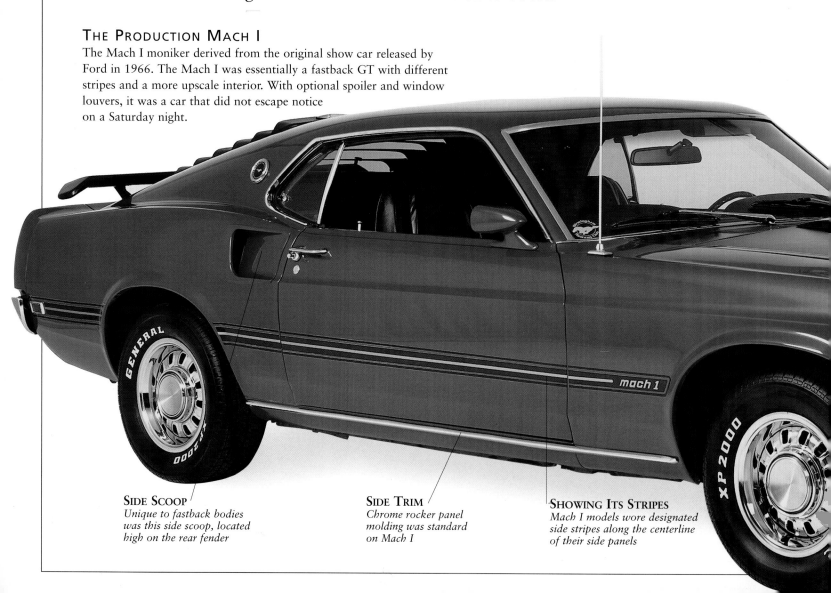

SIDE SCOOP
Unique to fastback bodies was this side scoop, located high on the rear fender

SIDE TRIM
Chrome rocker panel molding was standard on Mach I

SHOWING ITS STRIPES
Mach I models wore designated side stripes along the centerline of their side panels

NEW LOOK
Roof vents disappeared in 1969 and were replaced by a galloping-horse roof badge on fastback models

FASTBACKS ONLY
All Mach I models were of the fastback body style

COLOR KEYED
Racing-style mirrors matched the color of the car

STEEL WHEELS
The wheels were carried over from 1968 models

MACH MARKINGS

Mach I models had accent stripes around the upper portion of the rear body panel. All fastback models featured the kicked-up rear spoiler. Rear window louvers were optional.

HOOD SCOOP

The nonfunctional hood scoop showed an engine designation badge on both sides.

TURN HERE

Turn-signal indicators were on the back side of the hood scoop.

SHAKER HOOD SCOOP

An interesting option came in the 1969 model year. The shaker air scoop mounted on top of a special air cleaner and protruded through the hood. A vacuum-operated door opened when the throttle was floored, allowing cool air into the carburetor. The scoop was standard on the 428 Cobra Jet Ram-Air V-8 and optional for Mach I or GT with 351 or 390 engines. It was also available on the Boss 302. The name came from the fact that it shook when the engine was started or revved.

BLACKOUT HOOD
A major portion of the hood was blacked out to add a sinister look and reinforce the race car appearance

HOOD PINS
Hood pins further accented the Mach I's racing theme

AIR DAM
A front spoiler was bolted to the front roll pan, adding a "racing" touch

The shaker hood was for the buyer who wanted to intimidate the competition

1969 Mustang Variations

THE NEW ADDITIONS TO THE 1969 Mustang line reached out to every possible pony-car customer. Aimed at the high end of the market, Grandé models, available in coupe only, were more plush than the average Mustang and offered 45 options. Standard features included interior upgrades such as "Comfortweave" hopsack upholstery, simulated woodgrain dashboard, padded interior side panels, and extra-thick carpet on the floorboard. The most exciting addition was the first Boss Mustang, the 302, which was a hot-rodded fastback model equipped with a higher performance version of the 302cid engine. The exterior featured side striping, a partially blacked-out hood, front air dam, rear spoiler, and no side scoop on its rear fenders. On the heels of the 302 would come what is still considered the biggest, baddest, and meanest of all Mustangs – the Boss 429.

KEY FEATURES
1969 MUSTANG GRANDÉ

- **Production:** 22,182 units
- **Only available as a hardtop**
- **Luxury interior, including Rim Blow steering wheel standard**
- **Two-tone narrow side stripes**
- **Wire-style wheel covers**

1969 GRANDÉ
The Mustang Grandé was aimed at a more upscale nonperformance-minded buyer. It offered more standard comfort items, such as extra sound insulation and a special soft-ride suspension. Although the performance engines could be ordered, it was much tamer than a Mach I or Boss.

VINYL TOP
This was a popular Grandé option

STRIPES
A two-tone striping pattern was included in the Grandé package

SIDE MIRRORS
Racing-style mirrors were standard on Grandé

WHEELWELL TRIM
Trim was standard on Grandé; an option on other models

1969 BOSS 302

Introduced in late 1969, the Boss 302 was not in the standard sales brochure. This was a special car with racing in mind. Ford wanted to get approval for a revised 302 engine for Trans-Am racing, so a limited number of cars were built (1,628) to make it eligible for the series. These cars were built on the fastback body (without the side scoops) and included a blacked-out hood, trunk lid, and taillight panel. Special body side C-stripes and front chin spoiler rounded out the standard features. Popular options included the rear spoiler and rear window louvers. A tribute to their winning ways in the Trans-Am series, the street models are highly prized by collectors today.

The Boss 302 had its roots in Trans-Am racing – adding even more spice to the Mustang line

IDENTIFICATION
The emblem on the rear roof pillar is the only place the model is distinguished on the exterior of the car

ROCKER PANEL MOLDINGS
As with the Mach I, chrome moldings were standard

WHEEL COVERS
Simulated wire-style wheel covers were standard on the Grandé package, adding a touch of class

GRANDÉ FASHION
The Mustang Grandé came with a luxurious interior. Vinyl bucket seats featured cloth inserts and adjustable headrests. The door panels, center console, and dash were all trimmed with teak-toned appliques, and the doors had courtesy lights. Buyers had a choice of manual or automatic transmission.

1970 Mustang Boss 429

BOSS 429 LOGO

WHAT MANY CONSIDER the greatest Mustang ever made broke all the rules of production car street power. The Boss 429 contained a 429cid hemi-head V-8 engine that was so big it would not fit in the 1969 Mustang without modifications to the car's suspension. Ford set up a separate assembly line, where the mighty engine was squeezed into 859 fastbacks. The low production total reflected Ford's intentions, which were not originally to build a car like the Boss but to qualify its engine for NASCAR racing. To qualify, the engine had to be installed in street cars. In 1970 Ford produced only 499 Boss 429s, creating by the end of that year a car so unique and so rare as to achieve legendary status almost instantly. More than 30 years later, the Boss 429 remains one of the most sought-after Mustangs of all time.

KEY FEATURES
1970 BOSS 429 MUSTANG

- **Production:** 499 units
- **Largest engine ever offered**
- **Magnesium valve covers**
- **Large hood scoop**
- **Altered front suspension allowing for engine clearance**

MIGHTY MUSCLE
Arguably the king of all musclecars, the Boss 429 had the biggest engine ever offered in a Mustang. Because it was also produced in low numbers it is highly valued as a collectible car.

AIR SUPPLY
The Boss 429's hood scoop was the biggest ever placed on a production Mustang

AIR DAM
A front spoiler, similar to that on the Mach I, was added

FRONT SCOOP
A scoop on the front edge of the fender replaced the outer headlights in all 1970 Mustangs

WIDE TRACK
Boss 429 had a two-inch wider track to allow clearance for the engine

MAXIMUM KICK: THE BOSS 429 ENGINE

The Boss 429 engines of 1969–70 were developed for use in NASCAR racing. Sewer pipe–size intake ports assured adequate air flow for 8,000 rpm operation. Large-diameter valves were placed in the aluminum cylinder head at different angles, creating a near hemispherical combustion chamber that produced a more uniform burning of the fuel/air mixture. Several different camshafts, both solid and hydraulic lifters, were employed in an attempt to improve street performance, but the gargantuan ports made low-speed operation less than efficient. Four-bolt main bearing caps reduced crankshaft flexing at higher rpms, and an external oil cooler mounted on the core support ensured bearing life. A 780 CFM Holley carburetor mixed the premium fuel and air obtained via the hood-mounted scoop. All of this amounted to an advertised 375 hp, but in the hands of experienced racing engine builders, the output could exceed 500 hp.

Ford deemed the Boss 429 so radical that it added a supplement to the owner's manual

The 429 engine required so much space that the suspension had to be relocated and the battery had to be placed in the trunk

INTERIOR
The Boss 429 was only available with a white or black interior for 1970

PAINT
Grabber Blue (original on this example) was a popular color for 1970

BOSS TIRES
Boss 429s rode on Goodyear Polyglas F-60-15s, the largest tire to grace a production Mustang of the day

NEW LIGHTS
The taillight bezel reverted back to a one-piece unit for 1970.

DRESSED UP
Chrome Magnum 500 wheels were an upgrade from the standard steelies with "dog dish" hubcaps.

1970 Mustang Variations

AS THE MUSTANG ENTERED the second year of its third restyling, the most noticeable revision was the addition of a scooped fender cap next to the headlights, giving the nose an aerodynamic, simplified look. New vertical side markers matched the contour of the front grille. The fake exhaust trim that had gotten mixed reviews was eliminated in favor of a cleaner look. Supported by solid sales, the Mach I remained in the 1970 line, but the GT had fallen victim to the successful sales of the new high-performance Mustangs. The Mustang had record low sales in 1970. Total sales plunged to 190,727, down about 109,000 units from the year before. Even the bread-and-butter hardtop failed to sell more than 100,000 units, and the convertible did not crack the 10,000 mark. These sales figures were not reflecting lower quality or attractiveness, but rather an oversaturation of a highly competitive market.

> ### KEY FEATURES
> #### 1970 MUSTANG GRANDÉ
>
> - **Production:** 22,182 units
> - **Only available as a hardtop**
> - **Luxury interior with hounds-tooth cloth seat inserts**
> - **Landau vinyl top standard**
> - **Wire-style wheel covers now optional**

1970 MUSTANG GRANDÉ
The 1970 Grandé was still geared toward the upscale buyer. Updates for this year included revised interior patterns, a landau style vinyl top and a stylish set of slotted steel wheels.

NEW BADGE
For 1970 the Grandé emblem changed from block letters to script

VINYL TOP
A three-quarter landau top was standard on the 1970 Grandé

NO SCOOP
A scoop would not reappear here until 1994

UNIQUE WHEEL
Only 1970 Mustangs and Mercurys had this stamped, five-slot wheel

SETTING THE PACE

Although its sales were way down, the Mustang had one of its best racing seasons in 1970 and was chosen as the official pace car of Michigan Speedway. Shown here are a Mach I and convertible specially prepared for the occasion.

1970 TWISTER SPECIAL

Ford made a special version of the Mach I for Kansas dealerships called the Twister Special. Only 96 cars were produced, making them extremely rare today.

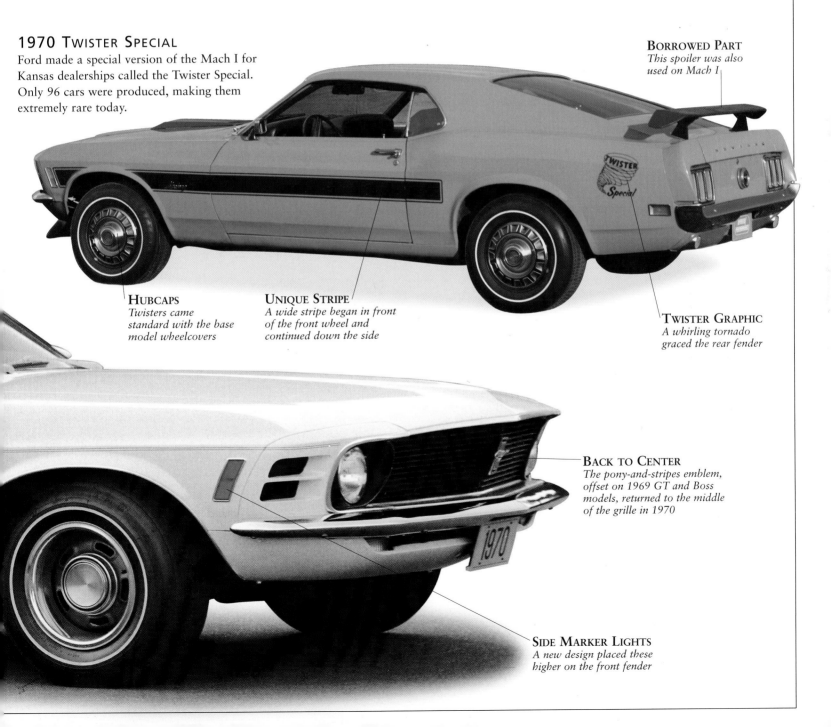

BORROWED PART
This spoiler was also used on Mach I

HUBCAPS
Twisters came standard with the base model wheelcovers

UNIQUE STRIPE
A wide stripe began in front of the front wheel and continued down the side

TWISTER GRAPHIC
A whirling tornado graced the rear fender

BACK TO CENTER
The pony-and-stripes emblem, offset on 1969 GT and Boss models, returned to the middle of the grille in 1970

SIDE MARKER LIGHTS
A new design placed these higher on the front fender

Trans-Am Victory

IN THE 1970 TRANS-AM RACING SERIES, Ford's main objective was to beat Chevrolet. Carroll Shelby had retired from racing in 1968, leaving Ford with team owner Bud Moore and drivers Parnelli Jones and George Follmer. With cars restricted to one carburetor by Trans-Am rules, Moore prepared a single four-barrel manifold, dubbed the "Mini-Plenum," that produced 450 hp with a power band range from 3,500 to 8,000 rpm. The Camaro was going through first-year redesign growing pains, so the real battle was fought with Mark Donahue in an AMC Javelin. Jones took the drivers' championship and Follmer finished third, sandwiching Donahue at second place. The Mustangs won six of the eleven races and finished second in five. Mustang won the Trans-Am Manufacturers' Cup with 72 points to the Javelin's 59 and Camaro's 40. Ford pulled out of motorsports after the 1970 season, not to return with any degree of commitment until the early 1980s.

BUD MOORE
Bud Moore ponders his next racing decision. His drivers, Parnelli Jones and George Follmer, were almost unbeatable throughout the season.

1970 BOSS 302 TRANS-AM MUSTANG
This is one of the race cars Bud Moore prepared specially for the 1970 Trans-Am racing season. Here Parnelli Jones gets ready to race in the Number 15 Boss 302 Mustang.

ON THE RIGHT TRACK
Ford Mustang driver George Follmer, who took nine top fives out of eleven races in 1970, charges toward a turn in one of the Boss 302 cars.

HARD CHARGERS
George Follmer and Parnelli Jones running one and two at Laguna Seca. Their team, owned by Bud Moore, easily won the championship even though Ford's racing fund was running out of money.

IN THE WINNER'S CIRCLE
Parnelli Jones at Laguna Seca, after one of six race wins for Ford Mustang in 1970, the year they pulled out of motorsports. Jones won the drivers' championship that year.

1969–1970 Memorabilia

MUSTANG COLLECTORS CAN CHOOSE from a wealth of items relating to 1969–70 models. Not only did Ford introduce racy new cars such as the Boss and Mach I, but toy and model manufacturers also have reproduced these Mustangs in a wide range of formats. Both Boss and Mach I Mustangs have been replicated in small scale and offered as promotional models, die-casts, and model kits. Toys such as the popular Hot Wheels by Mattel are also available, and those produced in 1969–70 command impressive prices at swap meets and toy shows.

MODEL KITS
Kits continued to be popular, with the older ones being most sought after. The original Revell kit depicting a gold car (shown here) included a mail-order offer for the "Pony Tale" record featured below.

PONY TALE
Manufactured by Revell in 1969, this record featured interviews with Peter Brock, a journalist who worked with Carroll Shelby, and Skip Hess, one of the Mustang Boss designers. The record was offered by Revell as a premium.

CARTOON MODELS

A cartoonlike 1969 Mustang "funny car" was produced via a partnership between Monogram and Mattel's Hot Wheels brand. The kit featured a car with caricatured proportions molded in color and a separate "painting" of the box art. Model kits of cartoon cars such as this were very much in style at the time.

LITERATURE

A 1969 dealer's brochure cover showed a closeup of the front drivers side of the new Mach I. The 1969–70 owner's manual featured a psychedelic pattern – a sign of the time.

DETAILED BOSS

This replica of a 1970 Boss 302 was made in Italy and sold under the Mattel name. A fairly detailed replica for its time, it featured opening doors, trunk, and hood, and it came with a display case.

PERFORMANCE ADS

Performance was the theme of 1969–70. This ad for the Boss 429 shows a dragster smoking the tires. A different ad told buyers that Mach I really meant "Mach Won."

BUMP 'N' GO

Taiyo of Japan sold this 1969 Mustang replica. Made of tin, its selling slogan was "Non-Fall Mystery Bump 'n' Go." The toy was powered by batteries and could crash into a wall, back up, turn around, and find something else to hit.

4

THE SHELBY YEARS

1965–1970

1965 to 1970 marked a special time for the Mustang. A joining of forces between racing legend Carroll Shelby and Ford resulted in some of the most desirable Mustangs to hit the streets. The 1967 Shelby GT500 (above and left) is a splendid example of the Shelby-Ford era.

The Shelby-Ford Alliance

SHELBY MUSTANGS ARE MORE than an important part of Ford history – they hold a legendary place in the history of the American sports car. Although the alliance between Ford and Carroll Shelby spanned only five years, the partnership produced some of the most impressive performance cars in the world. The first Shelby GT350 debuted in 1965. The next five years saw two major design changes, both of which added weight and comfort. But Ford placed increasingly heavy demands on Shelby and his California

Carroll Shelby in 1969, standing among three of his creations

facility, which had been set up to make the vehicles. Corporate pressure from Ford went against the grain of a man who cherished racing above all other interests. And by 1969, sales were slowing. By mutual agreement, the Shelby Mustang project ended. Ford updated the remaining '69 inventory to 1970 specifications and sold the vehicles as 1970 models.

The Shelby Era 1965–1970

Pre-1965: The Cobra	1965: The GT350	1966: The GT350H
Carroll Shelby dreamed of a sports car that was lightweight and had a powerful V-8 engine to compete with the European sports cars of the day. He made his dream a reality by combining England's AC Ace with the new Ford 260 engine: the AC Cobra.	After much racing success with his Cobras, Shelby was asked to modify the Mustang fastback into a world-class racer, and the GT350 was born.	Much to the surprise of Ford and Shelby, Hertz ordered 1,001 GT350s for their "Rent-a-Racer" program. Just $17 a day, or $70 a week, could buy a spot in the drivers seat of a GT350 Shelby Mustang.

AC Cobra brochure	*GT350s preparing to race*	*GT350H Hertz "Rent-a-Racer"*

People Behind the Mustang

CARROLL SHELBY

Carroll Shelby was born in Leesburg, Texas, on January 11, 1923. After high school, he joined the Army Air Corps and served during World War II as a flight instructor and test pilot. He was successful as a race car driver throughout much of the 1950s, winning several national driving titles within the United States as well as the 24 Hours of Le Mans in 1959. Soon after, in 1960, Shelby was forced to retire from driving due to a heart condition. In the early '60s, Shelby envisioned a race car that would combine the long-nosed design of a European sports car with the torque-producing power of an American V-8. He convinced the British company AC Cars to let him design a car on its existing

Carroll Shelby, a former race car driver, made the Mustang roar

chassis using Ford's 260 V-8. The Cobra sports car was launched, earning Shelby the nickname "The Snake." Shortly after the Mustang was introduced, Ford called on Shelby to build racing versions. After a failed attempt to buy the Italian company Ferrari, Ford sought to compete on the track with its own thoroughbred racing vehicle. By September 1964, Shelby had built the GT350 prototype, and within a year those cars were winning on the racing circuits. The GT350, which also sold as a production car, was embraced by the racing-enamored public. The agreement between Carroll Shelby and Ford Motor Company may have lasted only five years, but the cars produced during that time continue to survive as legends.

1967: The GT500

Shelby took advantage of the newfound space under the hood of Ford's newly designed '67 Mustang. The only Mustangs with 428 engines were Shelby's GT500s.

1967 GT500 428cid engine

1968: The GT500KR

Ford wanted a different kind of Shelby for 1968 based on a theory that a more comfortable car would sell better than a stripped-down racer. Shelby came up with the GT500KR. This year also marked the first Shelby convertibles offered in mass numbers.

1968 GT500 convertible

1969–1970: The End

By 1969, conflicting goals rocked the successful alliance between Ford and Shelby. Shelby's vision of a race car built for the masses had evolved into a performance-luxury car that could be seen cruising more than racing. Following poor sales in 1969, the Shelby Mustang project ended.

1969 GT500 convertible

1965 Shelby GT350

G.T. 350

1965 GT350 SIDE
MARKINGS

THE SHELBY MUSTANG WAS FIRST REVEALED to the public in January 1965. Dubbed the Shelby GT350, it was the first race-equipped car to be marketed to the public by a major American automobile company. All 1965 Shelbys were fastback models, but even among Shelbys the 1965 Shelby GT350 was unique because it came closer to being a true race car than the models that followed. The interior had no rear seat. In its place was a special fiberglass floor, and the spare tire was mounted just beneath the rear glass. The engine was Ford's 289cid, 271 hp Hi-Po, modified to add an extra 35 hp. Only 562 of the 1965 Shelby GT350s were built. Of this total, 516 were street models with a base price of $4,547, a steep figure for its day. The remaining 46 cars were Shelby GT350 "R" models specially built for road racing. These cars produced instant results on the racing circuit and enhanced the image of the Ford Mustang as a performance vehicle.

WHEELS
Cragar five-spoke wheels with special center caps were optional on 1965 Shelby GT350s.

A NEW BREED
The first of the Shelby breed set a whole new standard for muscle cars. The 1965 models are rare today because only 562 cars were produced.

RACING MIRROR
These mirrors were dealer-installed and mounted on either the fender or the door

HOOD
The fiberglass hood had a functional air scoop and racing pins

SHELBY GRILLE
The front end sported an offset Mustang side emblem on a simple honeycomb mesh screen

SIDE MARKING
The side-stripe n was derived from GT40 race car

WORLD CLASS
The GT350 "R" (racing) raced overseas as well, shown here at Le Mans. It also won stateside, taking victories in SCCA's B production from Lime Rock in Connecticut to Willow Springs in California.

HARD CHARGER
A GT350 "R" races one of Ford's GT40s in the 24 Hours of Daytona.

SPECIFICATIONS

MODEL SHOWN	1965 Shelby GT350 Mustang
PRODUCTION	562 units (including GT 350R)
BODY STYLES 1965–70	Fastback and convertible
CONSTRUCTION	Unibody chassis/body
ENGINES	289cid V-8 (1965–67) 302cid V-8 (1968) 351cid V-8 (1969–70) 428cid V-8 (1967–68) 428cid V-8 Cobra Jet (1968–70)
POWER OUTPUT	306 hp (289cid V-8) to 355 (428cid V-8)
TRANSMISSION	Four-speed manual
SUSPENSION	Independent front with coil springs; semielliptic leaf springs at rear; Koni shocks
BRAKES	Drums standard, discs optional on front
MAXIMUM SPEED	132 mph (212 km/h) (428cid) 0–60 mph (0–96 km/h) 6.7 seconds (428cid) 0–100 mph (0–161 km/h) 16.9 seconds (428cid) A.F.C. 10 mpg

TWO SEATER
The rear seat was removed so the GT350 would meet SCCA racing requirements

LOUVERS
1965 would mark the only year that the roof vents did not change

SIDE EXHAUST
Exhaust pipes were fitted with two-inch Glaspak mufflers and exited out the side

WHITE ONLY
1965 Shelbys were only available in Wimbledon White with a black interior

DASHBOARD
Among modifications to the interior were a custom three-spoked steering wheel and an instrument pod that housed a tachometer and oil pressure gauge. The design of the steering wheel did not include a horn, so it was relocated to the dash and activated by a switch. Rounding out the package were three-inch racing-style seatbelts.

1966 Shelby GT350H

1966 COBRA EMBLEM

WHEN THE SHELBY WAS INTRODUCED in 1965, Ford did not expect the car to be profitable. As it turned out the Shelby GT350 was not only well received but also successful at the race track. Ford dealers contended that the company could sell more Shelby Mustangs if the cars were more consumer-friendly and comfortable. This meant returning the back seat in the 1966 model and offering more color options. The biggest coup for Ford came when The Hertz Corporation ordered 1,001 of the Shelby GT350s to offer as rentals. This single transaction nearly doubled sales of the Shelby for the year. These rental cars, which displayed special GT350H side markings, became known as "Rent-a-Racers," because customers rented them for a weekend of fast driving on streets and even drag strips. The 1966 year ended with 2,380 Shelby GT350s produced.

KEY FEATURES

1966 Shelby GT350H

- **Production:** 1,001 units
- **Ordered by The Hertz Corporation**
- **Special GT350H designation**
- **Plexiglass quarter windows**
- **New side scoops**

RENT-A-RACER
Most of the 1,001 Shelby Mustangs produced for Hertz wore black paint with gold striping. These models are now scarce because of the wear and tear they endured at the hands of weekend would-be race drivers.

TACHOMETER
Instead of the pod from 1965, 1966 had a dash-mounted tachometer

STRIPING
Rally stripes were a dealer-applied option for 1966 Shelby

STEEL HOOD
Hertz cars did not have the fiberglass hoods found on standard GT350s

FRONT GRILLE
The 1966 Shelby grille held the Mustang side crest instead of the corralled pony

WHEELS
Magnum 500 wheels with "Cobra" center caps were optional

REAR VIEW
The 1966 Shelby had a special gas cap featuring the GT350 emblem of a red, white, and blue cobra.

HERTZ MODEL
The "H" at the end of the GT350 designation identifies this as a Hertz model

BACKUP LIGHTS
GT350H, as well as the rest of the '66 Mustangs, featured standard backup lights

EMBLEM
All GT350s from 1965–66 had a "GT 350" badge beside the right taillight

REAR GLASS
Plexiglass replaced the louvers found on the 1965 model

SHELBY GT-350 289 ENGINE

The 1965–66 GT350s were powered by a modified version of Ford's already-potent 289. Starting with a Hi-Po 289, Shelby and his team added a high-rise aluminum intake manifold topped by a 715 cfm carburetor. A set of tuned tubular steel headers went nearly straight through two-inch glasspack mufflers. With these performance parts, power jumped from 271 hp to 306 hp. All of this performance would be dressed up in Shelby's soon-to-be-famous aluminum Cobra valve covers, oil pan, and chrome air cleaner.

SIDE EXHAUST
Many GT350H owners modified the exhaust system from the original rear-exiting design

SCOOPS
Functional fiberglass scoops cooled the rear brakes

The 289 engine in GT350s was tuned to make 305 hp

1967 Shelby GT500

1967 SHELBY
GAS CAP

The 1967 Ford Mustang was increased in size to accept larger engines. This enabled Shelby to add an all-new model to his line: the GT500. The Shelby GT350 kept the 289cid Hi-Po engine, while the GT500 was equipped with Ford's massive 428cid big-block engine. The car retained its fastback body style, but the cosmetic changes included a more aggressively designed one-piece fiberglass grille with high-beam headlights in its center and a Shelby emblem offset to the passenger side. The rear got a fiberglass spoiler, 1967 Mercury Cougar taillights, and a Shelby-labeled pop-open gas cap. Production of 1967 Shelby Mustangs totaled 3,225 units, an increase of more than 50 percent from the previous year. Much of this can be attributed to the 1967 Shelby's lower price and a greater level of comfort mandated by Ford.

ROLL BAR
The 1967 GT500 featured a padded roll bar and optional racing-style shoulder harnesses.

REAR SPOILER
The fiberglass rear spoiler reflected race-car trends of the day

SHELBY MUSCLE
This was the first Shelby Mustang powered by a big-block engine. The 428cid V-8 was rated a 355 hp, making this the most powerful Shelby on the street.

TWO SCOOPS
1967 Shelby was the first to get scoops on both the side panels and roof

TEN SPOKES
Special Shelby ten-spoke wheels were an option

428CID BIG-BLOCK ENGINE

One reason the 1967 Mustang was made larger was to accept larger engines. True to Shelby form, these engines received modifications for increased performance. Twin Holley 650cfm carburetors were mounted atop the engine to increase gas intake, a special air cleaner allowed the engine to breathe easier, and tube headers were added for less restrictive exhaust flow. These modifications boosted the rated horsepower of the 428cid engine to 355 at 4,500 rpm. It should be noted that the 1967 GT500 was the first Mustang to receive the 428cid powerplant. The largest engine available in factory Mustangs for the year was the 390cid. It was not until 1968 that standard Mustangs would have the 428 installed.

Big-block GT500 models found ample power in the 428cid engine with dual carburetors

KEY FEATURES
1967 Shelby GT500

- **Production:** 2,048 units
- **First Mustang with 428 engine**
- **1967 Cougar taillights**
- **Extended fiberglass front fenders**
- **Molded fiberglass rear spoiler**

HOOD SCOOP
The fiberglass hood had a wide scoop with two openings

LE MANS STRIPES
The optional stripes were a popular addition to Shelby Mustangs

HOOD PINS
The hood was further secured by racing-style hood pins

HIGH BEAMS
Most 1967 Shelbys have their inner headlights located in the center of the grille like this, but lighting laws in some states dictated they be placed at the grille's outer edges.

NEW FASCIA
The fiberglass grille extended the length of the Shelby three inches longer than the factory Mustang

GRILLE EMBLEM
A special grille emblem sported either a GT350 or GT500 model designation

THE WINDOW SCOOP
1967 was the first year Shelby added a scoop to the area where the quarter window would go. These scoops provided fresh air to the occupants. The rear openings on these scoops were supposed to house rear-pointing lights as seen on the Shelby race cars of the day, but this feature was canceled due to federal regulations on the consumer cars.

1968 Shelby GT500KR

1968 GT500KR GAS CAP

1968 WAS THE MOST SUCCESSFUL year in the history of Shelby Mustang. For the first time the lineup included a convertible, and a racy new model called the GT500KR was unveiled. Cosmetic changes for this model year included a redesigned fiberglass nose piece with a grille opening that extended well below the front bumper. Set inside were a set of fog lamps, and above it was S-H-E-L-B-Y spelled out in block letters. The rear end also got a specially made fiberglass panel with 1965 Ford Thunderbird sequential taillights. The 289cid Hi-Po engine was replaced by the 302cid in GT350 models; GT500s retained the 428cid powerplant, this time with a single carburetor. Later in the year the GT500KR "King of the Road" made its debut. This racy, luxurious vehicle was powered by the high-performance 428cid Cobra Jet engine. Only 1,251 GT500KRs were ever produced.

KEY FEATURES
1968 Shelby GT500KR

- **Production:** 318 units (convertible)
- **First Shelby convertible offered**
- **1965 Thunderbird taillights**
- **Updated fiberglass front fenders and hood**
- **More luxurious interior**

COLLECTIBLE CONVERTIBLE
Shelby KR models were rare, but the convertible version was especially so. This car is one of the most collectible of all Shelby Mustangs, because only 318 were produced.

NEW PINS
Quarter-turn fasteners replaced the old-style hood pins in 1968

FOG LAMPS
The high-beam headlights were dropped in favor of fog lamps in the grille

FRESH AIR
The two frontal scoop openings forced air into the air cleaner

FRONT GRILLE
A massive opening was created by extending the grille below the bumper

MOLDING
GT500KRs featured chrome trim around their wheel wells

THUNDERBIRD TAILLIGHTS
1965 Thunderbird taillights were housed in the Shelby's rear panel.

COBRA JET
Only Shelbys with the Cobra Jet engine had this side emblem.

SIDE MARKINGS
The KR stood for "King of the Road"

SPOILER
1968 featured a fiberglass rear spoiler with "Shelby" block letters

WHEELS
Shelby ten-spoke cast-aluminum wheels continued to be an option

ROLL BAR
A special roll bar was installed in the GT500KR

ANTENNA
The convertible's radio antenna was mounted on the rear quarter panel

DELUXE OPTION
All 1968 Shelby models could be equipped with the Deluxe Interior Option available at extra cost on factory Mustangs.

COBRA JET POWER

Only Shelby GT500KR models came powered by the 428 Cobra Jet engine. Unlike previous powerplants found in Shelby Mustangs, the 428 Cobra Jet took on a stock appearance due in large part to its blue snorkeled air cleaner, although it still featured its "Cobra" valve covers. Fresh air was forced into the air cleaner through the functional hood scoop.

A rubber gasket sealed the Cobra Jet's air cleaner to the hood

MORE CHROME
GT500KRs had bright rocker panel moldings

ADDED COOLING
The scoop fed air to cool the rear brakes

SIDE MARKERS
Like other 1968 Mustangs, the Shelbys also sported side marker lights

1969–1970 Shelby GT500

1969 GT500
GRILLE EMBLEM

FORD MUSTANG WENT THROUGH its third restyle in 1969. With it came the most radical Shelby Mustang body treatments to date. The front fenders of Shelby GT350s and GT500s were special fiberglass units with built-in scoops that configured to accommodate a full-width grille. This foreshadowed the redesign of the Mustang for 1971, as would the NASA ducts on the hood. Three of these scoops faced forward and two faced back. The center scoop supplied air to the engine's intake system. The fastback model used the new Mach I Mustang body as a platform. The 302cid engine was replaced with Ford's new 351cid, 290 hp powerplant in GT350 models, while the GT500 continued with the 428 Cobra Jet at 335 hp.

SPECIAL WHEEL
All 1969 Shelby Mustangs came with custom-made, five-spoke cast-aluminum wheels with steel rims.

COBRA EMBLEM
The coiled snake graces the rear roof pillars

SPOILER
A fiberglass spoiler was mounted in the rear

MADEOVER MODEL
The 789 remaining 1969 Shelbys in Ford inventory after the model year were titled as 1970 models. These were modified to include a front air dam and a blackout point treatment around the outboard hood scoops.

SIDE SCOOPS
Functional side scoops provided air to the rear brakes

FENDERS
Front fenders were fiberglass for the first and only time

ROLL BAR
The bar was carried over from 1968 models

MIRRORS
Side mirrors could be equipped with optional remote control

BUCKET SEATS
High-back bucket seats were standard

1969 SHELBY GT500 CONVERTIBLE

Now aimed at the more upscale buyer, the GT500 convertible became more of an image car than a street/race car like the early models.

ILLUMINATION
Lucas fog lamps were mounted below the front bumper

FRONT GRILLE
The Mustang gets a full-width grille for the first time

SIDE EMBLEM
Fenders sported a new 428 Cobra Jet emblem

SIDE STRIPES
New for 1969 were stripes applied midway up the sides

QUICK RELEASE
Hood restraints were similar to 1968's quarter-turn fasteners

HOOD
Shelby continued to use fiberglass for the hood material

HOOD SCOOPS
The hood was vented with five inverted scoops called "NASA ducts"

KEY FEATURES

1969 Shelby GT500

- **Production:** 1,871 units
- Based on redesigned 1969 Mustang
- Updated fiberglass front fenders and hood
- Unique front bumper
- 1970 models were updated '69s

BRAKE SCOOPS
Scoops on fenders provided air to the brakes

NEW FACE
Shelby went to extremes to redesign the front end, which included this chrome-steel bumper

FRONT SCOOP

Fiberglass fenders had distinctive scoops molded in. For the first and only time, the model designation was moved from the lower body sides to the front fenders.

Shelby Memorabilia

1970 SHELBY OWNER'S MANUAL

BECAUSE THE SHELBY MUSTANGS were produced in limited numbers, most people will never have the chance to enjoy the experience of owning one. However, thanks to several manufacturers, you can purchase a miniature Shelby of your own. Carroll Shelby himself created a market for memorabilia collectors. He ran a Shelby mail-order business during the 1960s that sold many products, including performance parts, sportswear, and specialties. Shelby enthusiasts also consider dealer brochures, magazine ads, and other promotional literature desirable. Today, Carroll Shelby's name still graces a nationwide organization called the Shelby American Automobile Club (SAAC) and an official website that offers items for sale.

SHOW YOUR COLORS
Decals from SAAC are an easy way to show your Shelby enthusiasm.

VALVE COVER REPLICA
Among the most visible items under the hood of any Shelby Mustang were the Cobra aluminum valve covers. The originals can command a premium, but SAAC offers this replica in one-third scale.

CAST ALUMINUM
The cooling ribs replicate the original pattern

COBRA POWER
"Cobra powered by Ford" meant maximum performance in its day

SHELBYS IN SCALE

Today it is possible to have a Shelby collection of your own. Die-cast models ranging in scales and styles can help satisfy your desire to own a real Shelby, even several. Many rare cars are replicated, including a one-off '66 GT350S. The "S" stood for supercharged.

GT 350S
Only one car left the Shelby plant with a supercharger, and this die-cast model replicates it faithfully

GT350R
With only 34 full-scale cars produced and many destroyed in racing accidents, this die-cast model is the only way most people can have one

GT350
Accurate replicas of this favorite are available in scales from 1:43 to 1:12

SHELBY KITS
These AMT model kits produced in 1968 are hard to come by, with the Shelby Drag Team being extremely rare

The Hertz Sports Car Club features the G.T. 350-H
(The H is for Hertz)

IN THE MAIL
This postcard was distributed by Hertz to promote the GT350H

Order your Mustang as hot as you like

...even Shelby hot!

MUSTANG

People will talk...

Shelby GT 350 500

SHELBY LITERATURE
Ads and catalogs were all about performance. Highly collectible today, these are a must-have for the true Shelby collector.

SHELBY HOT
This Ford ad lets buyers know that the Mustang could be ordered mild to wild

SHELBY IMAGE
By 1969, the Shelby had become an image car as this ad shows

351 RAM AIR

5

THE TRANSITIONAL YEARS

1971–1973

In the early 1970s, Americans wanted their cars to be as comfortable as their homes. Mustang adapted and turned into a luxurious cruise machine like this 1971 model (above and left). It was the age of the gas-guzzler, but not for long. The tide was turning.

Muscle Gives Way at Last

AMERICA'S HEYDAY with fast, powerful, exciting cars was declining by 1971. Perhaps the heyday would have continued if political forces had not come into play, but pressure to increase the safety and fuel efficiency of automobiles had changed the marketplace. Following passage of the 1970 Federal Clean Air Act, automobile manfacturers were required to meet strict new safety and emissions standards, including the development within six years of engines that would eliminate 90 percent of exhaust emissions. Ford was forced to redirect its braintrust toward more politically correct missions, and the company abruptly pulled out of racing. The Mustangs of the early 1970s reflect an increase in size and the number of safety features, such as larger bumpers, that the times demanded. The 1971 model year would be the swan song for the big Boss Mustangs. Many would agree that the Mustang was entering a less interesting but necessary new era of design and performance.

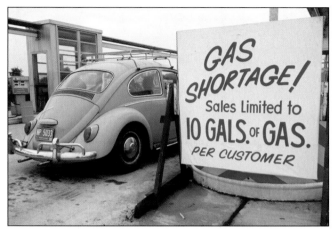

ENERGY CRISIS
Gasoline shortages in the 1970s would hasten the move toward smaller, more fuel-efficient transportation.

Cars & Culture 1971–1973

1971: Mustang Leads	1971: Last Boss	1972: Watergate
Ford's main competitors, the Chevrolet Camaro and Pontiac Firebird, had gone though major redesigns just eight months earlier. Their new look had an Italian flair, but they were still playing catch-up. Ford's new Mustang outsold the 1971 Camaro by nearly 25 percent.	Equipped with a 351 Cleveland engine rated at 330 hp, the Boss 351 did the quarter mile in 14.1 seconds at 100.6 mph. But the car was born too late. Emissions regulations killed it, and by 1972 it was gone.	In June 1972 Cuban exiles under orders of the President's re-election campaign broke into the Democratic National Committee headquarters. The Watergate scandal ensued, leading to the resignation of President Richard Nixon.

1971 Camaro	*The Mustang Boss 351*	*Watergate hearings*

People Behind the Mustang

LAWRENCE K. SHINODA

When most people hear the name of designer Larry Shinoda, they connect his days at Ford with the high-profile Boss 302 or Boss 429 and the racy styling packages he applied to those cars. However, he was equally involved in the design of the big Mustangs of the early 1970s. Born to Japanese parents in Los Angeles in 1930, Shinoda was a student at Burbank Junior High in 1942 when he was forced with his family into Manzanar internment camp in Owens Valley, California. He did not let that experience hold him down. After the war, Shinoda graduated from Art Center College of Design in Los Angeles and worked for Studebaker-Packard before joining General Motors, where he was known for designing the famous 1963 split-window Sting Ray Corvette. In 1968, he followed

Larry Shinoda, at his desk thinking "Boss" in 1970

Semon E. "Bunkie" Knudson to Ford, where, working closely with Knudson, the newly hired Ford president, Shinoda influenced the design of the 1971 Mustangs. This included the Kamm back end – a flat, chopped-off design originated by Wünibald Kamm in the 1930s. Shinoda worked at Ford Motor Company for a total of only 18 months but he left a big mark there as well as on the rest of the automotive world. Shinoda never stopped working; he died of a heart attack in 1997 while working in his home office. Shinoda is lauded for having spent his life creating innovative designs for snowmobiles, trucks, racing uniforms, and motor homes, and contributing to some of the most significant car designs in automotive history.

1972: Sprint

Ford released a special edition Mustang, called the Sprint, to commemorate the 1972 Olympic Games. About 800 fastback Sprints painted red, white, and blue were produced, plus 50 convertibles.

1972 Mustang Sprint

1973: Last Convertible

Although production would resume in the mid-1980s, government concerns about safety put a temporary end to all American-made drop-tops by 1975. Mustang convertible production stopped with the 1973 model.

1973 Mustang convertible

1973: Safety Bumpers

1973 legislation mandated that the front bumpers on all American-made cars be able to withstand a five-mph collision without damage. Ford Mustangs complied.

Mustang "crash" bumper

1971–1973 Concept

FORD DESIGNERS AND ENGINEERS began work on the fourth restyle of the Mustang in early 1967. The mission: bigger. By that time it had become obvious that Mustang would need the capacity for larger engines. Ford had been shoehorning big-block 429 engines into cars that were designed to accept small blocks, adding more weight to suspension systems that were not meant to carry the load. These limitations, along with an increased demand for more luxury, dictated that the Mustang be made larger and more accommodating for engine work, road handling, and comfort. Thus early concept models for 1971 were large even when compared to the 1969 model, which had represented the largest increase in size since Mustang's inception. What automotive designers could not foresee was that by 1971, reduced demand for high performance, combined with federal emissions standards and insurance rate surcharges, would kill larger engines altogether.

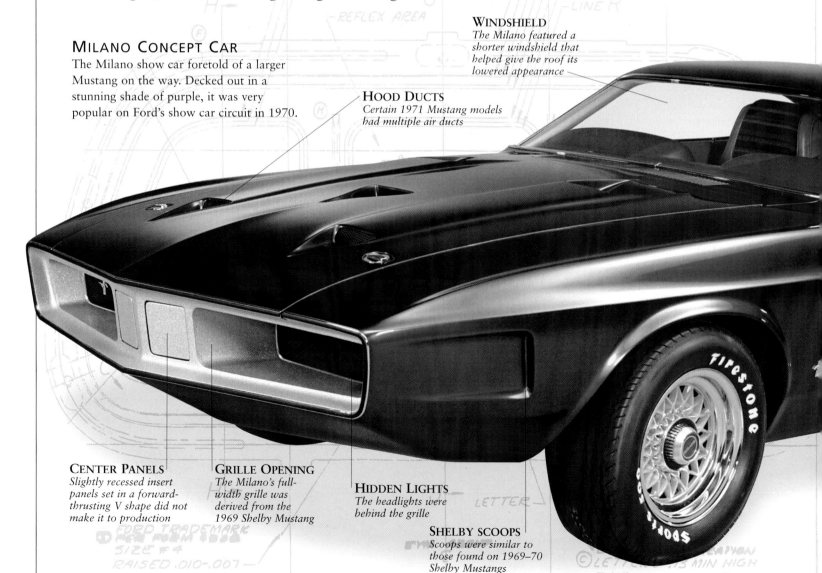

WINDSHIELD
The Milano featured a shorter windshield that helped give the roof its lowered appearance

MILANO CONCEPT CAR
The Milano show car foretold of a larger Mustang on the way. Decked out in a stunning shade of purple, it was very popular on Ford's show car circuit in 1970.

HOOD DUCTS
Certain 1971 Mustang models had multiple air ducts

CENTER PANELS
Slightly recessed insert panels set in a forward-thrusting V shape did not make it to production

GRILLE OPENING
The Milano's full-width grille was derived from the 1969 Shelby Mustang

HIDDEN LIGHTS
The headlights were behind the grille

SHELBY SCOOPS
Scoops were similar to those found on 1969–70 Shelby Mustangs

A REAL FASTBACK

Mustang Milano's rear roofline showed quite a bit of slope, a design that was carried over to the 1971 fastback model.

WINDOW
The rear window was nearly horizontal, making an obtrusive rear view

EXHAUST
Rectangular exhaust tips exited through the rear valance

TAILLIGHTS
These changed colors when the car was coasting (yellow), accelerating (green), or stopping (red), but this feature would not reach production

WHEELS
Lacy-style wheels would not make production, although a similar wheel would show up on future Mustangs

EMBLEM
Front fenders had a small pony-over-stripes badge with "Milano" in block letters

ROOFLINE
The Milano sported a racy fastback roof design

DOOR HANDLES
Milano did not have conventional outside handles; doors were opened electronically

WIDE BODY
Added inches outside allowed for more comfort inside

PAINT
A custom Ultra Violet paint job was a hit at the auto shows

MILANO INTERIOR

The Milano's plush interior offered a higher comfort level, one of the key objectives for 1971 Mustang. The dash was similar to those found in the 1969–70 models but it was covered in high-fashion purple leather trimmed with wood-grain inserts. The seats were the same purple leather used on the dash with striped cloth inserts. Matching purple luggage was stored where the back seat would be.

1971 Mustang Mach I

1971 POP-OPEN
GAS CAP

FOR 1971, THE MUSTANG was again offered in coupe, convertible, and fastback models. Despite the apparent boost in size, the car's 109-inch wheelbase was just 1 inch larger than that of the previous Mustang. The overall length grew slightly more than 2 inches, but the width saw an approximate 3-inch increase. Dimensional increases added more than 250 pounds to the Mustang, the largest weight gain in the car's history. The 1971 model was designed to accept Ford's new big-block "385 series" (429cid) engine, which was only available in that model year. The Mach I returned as the performance car, but performance was quickly becoming a thing of the past as tougher emissions and safety laws were taking effect. By late in 1971 it was obvious the musclecar was a thing of the past.

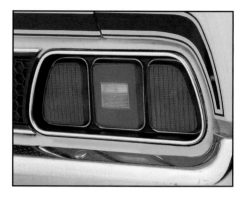

EVER-CHANGING TAILLIGHT
A new taillight bezel debuted in 1971. This would mark the fourth taillight design change in six years of production.

LAST OF A BREED
The Mach I returned bigger in 1971. It still played the musclecar role well with its bold stripes, spoilers, and available big-block engine. Limited sightlines through the back and side windows prompted reviewers to compare the car to a bunker.

MIRRORS
Ford's popular racing-style side mirrors were near carry-overs from last year's model

RAM AIR
A "NASA" hood with ducts that delivered fresh air to the engine was optional

NEW MARKINGS
Mach I got a new logo for the front fenders

BUMPER
Mach I had a color-keyed front bumper

FRONT SPOILER
The optional front spoiler gave the front a more aggressive appearance

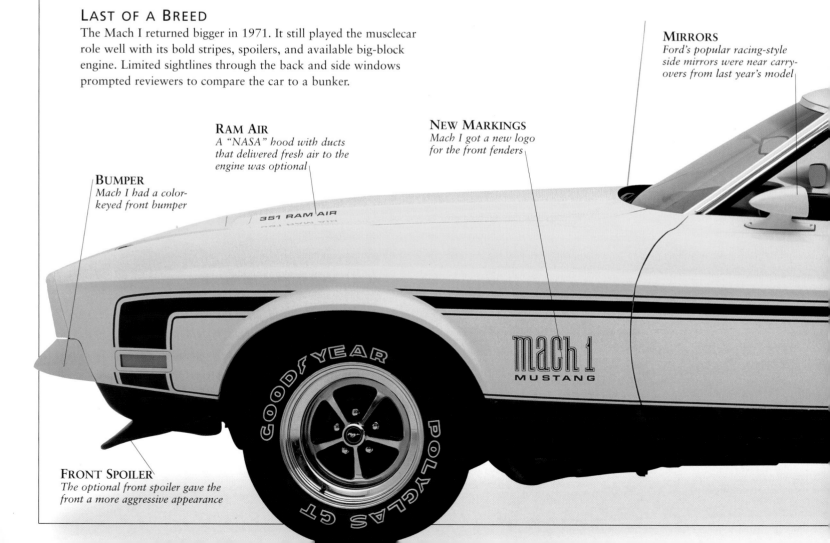

SPECIFICATIONS

MODEL SHOWN	1971 Mustang Mach 1
PRODUCTION	36,499 units
BODY STYLES 1971–73	Coupe, convertible, and fastback
CONSTRUCTION	Unibody chassis/body
ENGINES	250cid I-6 (1971–73) 302cid V-8 (1971–73) 351cid V-8 (1971–73) 351cid V-8 Cobra Jet (1971–73) 351cid V-8 Boss (1971) 429cid V-8 Cobra Jet (1971)
POWER OUTPUT	145 hp (250cid I-6) to 375 hp (429cid V-8)
TRANSMISSION	Three- and four-speed manual or three-speed automatic
SUSPENSION	Independent front with coil springs and wishbones; semielliptic leaf springs at rear
BRAKES	Drums standard, discs optional on front
MAXIMUM SPEED	108 mph (177–204 km/h) (302cid) 0–60 mph (0–96 km/h) 8.1 seconds (302cid) 0–100 mph (0–161 km/h) 24.6 seconds (302cid) A.F.C. 16 mpg (210 hp V-8)

A 351 WITH 285 HORSES

Ford offered two versions of the 351cid small-block engines in 1971 Mustangs. A 285 hp version was the optional small block for the Mach 1. A 330 hp was only available for the muscular Boss 351. The 285 hp 351 was a nice step for those who wanted a little more power than the 210 hp 302, but a little less than the kick of the Boss.

The 285 hp 351cid engine

WIDER ALL AROUND
The 1971 Mustang broke tradition with a full-width grille but reclaimed its original honeycomb pattern.

REAR STYLING
Mach I featured a honeycomb appliqué between the taillights; in the center was a then traditional pop-open gas cap.

LOW VISIBILITY
The roofline on the fastback model sloped at a 14-degree angle, making it difficult to back up the car

SPOILER
A rear spoiler was a popular option for the Mach I

SUSPENSION
Standard on the Mach I was a "competition suspension"

BLACKED OUT
Mach I featured black or argent painted lower body sides

1971 Mustang Variations

THE 1971 MUSTANG LINE was loaded with popular models from the previous year. Standard coupe, convertible, and fastback models came with a 250cid inline six-cylinder base engine. The Mach I, available only in the fastback body style, was the designated recipient of the large 429 engine, although the base engine was the small-block 302. Carrying on the performance trend, the Boss 351 debuted in 1971. It was equipped with a 330 hp version of the 351cid's powerplant and fitted with a functional Ram Air hood. The Mustang coupe could be upgraded to the Grandé model, which continued as the luxury leader of the line. Grandé came with a full vinyl top and special emblems on the rear-roof pillars. All engine options were available. The Grandé interior included a two-spoke steering wheel, wood-grain appliqués on the dash, Lambeth cloth seat inserts, electric clock, and rear ashtray.

> ### KEY FEATURES
>
> 1971 Mustang Coupe
>
> - Production: 65,696 units
> - Concealed windshield wipers
> - Coupe continued to be the top seller
> - Flush mounted door handles
> - "Reversible" keys

1971 MUSTANG COUPE
The Mustang was bigger, but sales did not follow. Reflecting a nearly 10-percent drop in sales, 65,696 standard model coupes like the one shown here were sold during the model year.

HIDDEN WIPERS
The 1971 featured a new design that placed the windshield wipers below the hood for a much cleaner look

PLAIN HOOD
Compared to the Mach I, the base model had a relatively flat hood

STANDARD GRILLE
The grille on standard models featured the corralled pony with horizontal side bars

TURN SIGNALS
Turn-signal indicators were mounted below the headlights

BETTER VIEW

Unlike the Mach I of the same model year, the rear window of the coupe had a more vertical slant so visibility was much improved.

GAS CAP
Base model Mustangs did not receive the pop-open gas cap that the Mach I had

REAR PANEL
This area was painted black and did not feature the honeycomb pattern used on the Mach I

BLOCK LETTERS
All standard 1971 Mustangs used block letters across the rear of the car

TIRES
Dual whitewall stripes added a little flash over the standard E78-14 blackwall tires

EMBLEM
The side emblem was similar to those found on 1968–70 models

EASY WINDOWS
For the first time power windows were an option on Mustangs

HUBCAPS
Slotted hubcaps with large polished centers adorned base model Mustangs

SIDE MIRRORS
Standard side mirrors were simple chrome units

DOOR HANDLES
Rectangular door handles flush mounted on the body were new for 1971

THE LAST BOSS

The Boss 302 and 429 for 1969–70 were the inspiration for the Boss 351 of 1971. Perhaps the most underrated musclecar of the era, the Boss 351 used the 351 Cleveland engine with modifications to pump output to 330 hp. The rest of the package included many of the standard Mach I features, as well as a functional NASA hood and body side stripes with "Boss 351" identification. New emissions regulations nearly killed the Boss 351 before it even went into production. Only 1,806 models were produced before the car disappeared for the 1972 model year.

Produced for 1971 only, the Boss 351 carried the torch passed on by the Boss cars of '69 and '70

1972 Mustang

CHANGES TO THE 1972 MUSTANG were almost undetectable from the outside. The new model had a Mustang script on the right side of the rear deck lid in place of the block lettering used on the previous model. For the first time (excluding the short carryover from the $1964^{1}/_{2}$ to 1965 model), Ford made no changes to the front grille or taillights. The company was preoccupied with engine adjustments. Federal emissions standards made it impossible for Ford to tame the big-block engines, and the smaller engines had to be modified to meet the new regulations. The largest engine available for 1972 was the 351CJ, and its performance decreased due to the emissions-related equipment.

KEY FEATURES

1972 Mustang Grandé

- Production: 18,045 units
- New hubcaps
- Revised rear script
- Vinyl top standard
- Low-compression engines

1972 GRANDÉ COUPE

The Grandé coupe continued to appeal to upscale buyers and from 1971–72 was one of the least visually changed cars in Mustang history. Ford had shifted its focus from design creativity to bringing its engines into compliance with new government regulations.

TOP
Vinyl tops continued to be standard on Mustang Grandé

DEFROST
First appearing on 1971 models, an optional rear-window defroster could be ordered on all coupe models

NEW SCRIPT
About the only way to tell a 1972 from a 1971 model is this script that replaced the block letters on the previous model

NO MORE MACH SPEED

The Mach I suffered as its standard 302 dropped to 140 hp from 210 hp in 1971. Government regulations required the engine-power measure to change from "gross" to "net." While actual power did not drop this far, the car's image did.

UNDER THE HOOD
Mach I was no longer available with the powerful big-block engines

WHEELS
Smooth hubcaps with trim rings were standard on 1972 Mach I

MACH MARKINGS
Mach I markings were carried over from the 1971 models

STRIPES
Continuing the Grandé tradition, painted body stripes were standard

WHEELCOVERS
New for 1972 was a set of stylish wheelcovers for the Grandé

MORE CHROME
All models except Mach I came with chrome rocker panel molding

MUSTANG CELEBRATED THE OLYMPICS

Although few changes came with the 1972 Mustang, a special edition, dubbed the Sprint, was released to celebrate the Olympic games that year. Sprint models were decked out with a patriotic red, white, and blue paint scheme. The mostly white body had a blue stripe from front to rear on its lower side panels and a USA shield decal on the rear fenders. Hardly Olympians in the performance category, Sprint models received no preferential engine treatment. Approximately 800 Sprint models were produced in the fastback body style, and a special run of 50 convertibles was offered in the Washington, DC, and Virginia area. Ford also offered Sprint models of their smaller Mavericks and Pintos.

The Sprints showed their spirit with red, white, and blue color schemes and special emblems commemorating the Olympics

1973 Mustang

THE STANDARD
1973 GRILLE EMBLEM

THE MUSTANG OF 1973 was the last of the largest Mustangs, and the last of the "first generation." By the time it was produced, American car buyers had shifted their preferences toward smaller cars. Thus, Ford saw little reason to pump money into modifications. The most noticeable changes were in the front end, with an extended bumper, vertical turn signals, and a larger egg-crate pattern in the grille fascia. Vertical grille bars emanated from the front emblem on standard cars. The decor package offered an additional option from which to choose. Chrome headlight and taillight bezels were standard for the year. The 1973 convertible would be the last drop-top Mustang Ford would produce for the next ten years.

ADDED DASH
The dashboard of the 1973 Mustang featured a two-spoke steering wheel. Large round gauges were easily visible.

THE LAST OF THE CONVERTIBLES
The 1973 model year would mark the end of the original Mustang convertible. Government concerns about safety would put an end, at least temporarily, to all American-made convertibles.

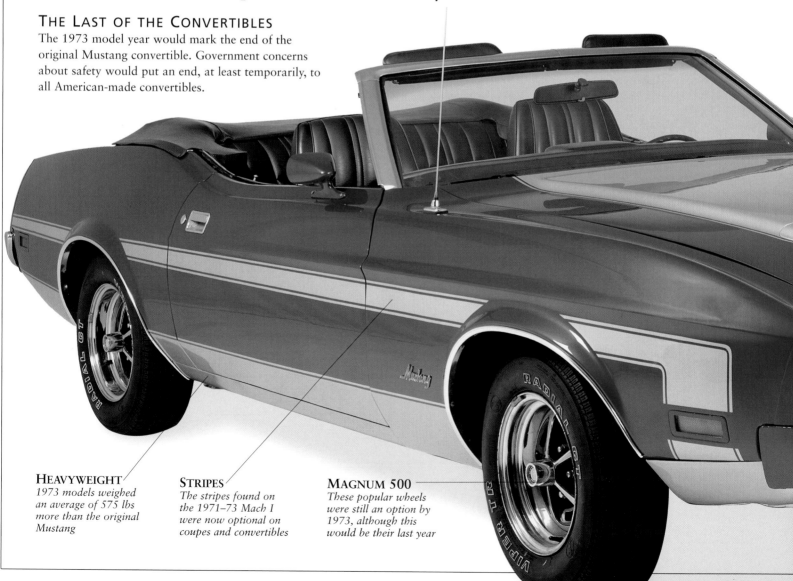

HEAVYWEIGHT
1973 models weighed an average of 575 lbs more than the original Mustang

STRIPES
The stripes found on the 1971–73 Mach I were now optional on coupes and convertibles

MAGNUM 500
These popular wheels were still an option by 1973, although this would be their last year

OUT IN GRANDÉ FASHION

The Grandé continued on in 1973 as the luxury version of the Mustang, although its days were numbered. With an all-new Mustang on the horizon, the Grandé model would not be carried over to the new car. Not many modifications were made for 1973 – only a few new colors were available and the new federally mandated front bumpers were added. Ford sold 25,274 units in 1973, the best year the Grandé ever had.

1973 would mark the last year for the Grandé

1973 MACH I

With so many other Mustang models being discontinued after this model year, it was nice to know the Mach I name would live on.

NEW WHEELS
Five-hole forged-aluminum wheels were optional on Mach I

NO MORE POP
By 1973, the Mach I had lost its pop-open gas cap

NEW STRIPES
Mach I for 1973 featured a stripe package that included this rear stripe and revised side graphics

NASA HOOD
The optional NASA hood had its roots in the aerospace industry

A NEW TURN
Turn signals on the 1973 model were vertical units located inside the grille opening

DECOR GROUP
As in 1972, the decor group option included a black grille with a small horse emblem

BEEFIER BUMPER
The color-keyed bumper was extended four inches to meet federal safety standards; the rear bumper was extended almost two inches

KEY FEATURES

1973 Mustang Convertible

- Production: 11,853 units
- New hubcaps
- New safety bumpers
- Vinyl top standard
- Low-compression engines

1971–1973 Memorabilia

THE 1971–73 MODELS WERE hot items for toy manufacturers. Companies such as Hot Wheels included them in their line of offerings, and AMT and MPC offered 1971 Mustang kits. Typically, the swooping fastback model claimed most of the attention. Promotional models were available to customers through dealers, and these are now among the most desired collectibles from the period. As always, for the serious Mustang enthusiast, dealer brochures and advertisements promoting the 1971–73 model years are required collectibles. As might be expected for these larger-than-average Mustangs, printed advertisements focused on driving comfort and luxury. One of Ford's most well-known advertising campaigns, "Ford has a better idea," was launched during this period. Ironically, Ford's better idea would be an all-new Mustang for 1974.

SHIFT KNOB
This 1971–73 optional Hurst shift knob is considered a collectible today.

WHEEL VARIETY
Brochures are a sure way to see exactly what wheels came on a certain year Mustang

OPTIONS GALORE
This is a good way to find out what options a car could have included

SAFTEY FEATURE LIST
Saftey became a major selling point, and this 1971 brochure lists all the saftey features

1971–1973 DEALER BROCHURES
These could be considered the most collectible, because these years are the earliest that have not been reprinted. Besides giving useful information about a particular model year, they provide interesting insight to the styles of the day.

MODEL KITS

As the Mustang got bigger in size, model kits of the 1971–73 became harder to come by. A rare find is the original issue '71 Mach I kit shown here. The Otaki kit shown here suffers from some inaccuracy, but the original issue is prized by kit collectors and Mustang enthusiasts alike.

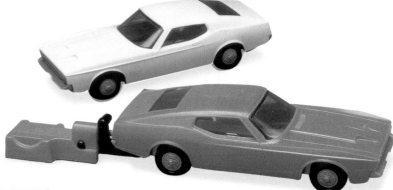

PROMOTIONALS

Ford dealerships often gave out promotional models to help "seal the deal" for a potential car buyer. As the 1970s approached, however, this practice decreased. Mustang promos of this era often bring several hundred dollars from collectors today.

SHOOTERS

These two miniature Mustangs came in Procter and Gamble detergent boxes of the mid-1970s. Replicating a 1973 Mustang, these were marketed as "Funmates" and featured a spring-loaded trigger device that shot the car across the floor.

Ford T5 Mach 1

T 5 Mach 1 – das ist die knappe Formel für sportliches und anspruchsvolles Autofahren. So nüchtern die Bezeichnung klingt, so aufregend ist das, was sich dahinter verbirgt.

Da ist die rasante Form, die die geballte Kraft verrät, die in diesem Auto steckt! Ein drehmomentstarker 4,9-Liter-V8-Motor mit 152 DIN-PS ist serienmäßig. Den noch stärkeren 5,7-Liter-V8-Motor mit 202 DIN-PS gibt es auf Wunsch.

Die gewaltige Kraft dieser V8-Motoren wird über superbreite Hochgeschwindigkeitsreifen auf die Straße gebracht. Rasante, farbabhängige Rennspiegel sorgen für gute Sicht nach hinten. Der Spiegel der

Fahrerseite ist von innen verstellbar. Die vordere Stoßstange ist als Spoiler ausgebildet, so daß der Fahrtwind diesen schweren Sportwagen bei hohen Geschwindigkeiten noch stärker auf die Straße preßt.

Die Innenausstattung ist die gekonnte Synthese aus sportlicher Sachlichkeit und exklusivem Luxus. Sportliche, aber dennoch komfortable Sitze mit hochgezogener Rückenlehne, dazwischen die markante Schalthebel des gut abgestuften Dreigangetriebes und eine breite Mittelkonsole mit praktischem Ablagefach. Eine breite Skala von Zusatzausstattungen und Extras gibt Ihnen die Möglichkeit, dem Interieur des Mach 1 schließlich noch Ihr ganz persönliches Gepräge zu geben.

ADS AND PROPAGANDA

Ford was still touting Mustang performance as this ad (above) from 1971 shows, although by the end of the year, Ford and all other auto manufacturers would be changing their tune. German propaganda featuring the T-5 is extremely rare in the US. This flyer from 1971 (left) features the "T-5 Mach 1" using the Mach 1 photo from the US Mustang brochure retouched into a German T-5.

6
THE REINVENTION YEARS

1974–1978

The Mustang was reinvented in 1974. Born out of the ashes of the early-1970s land-yachts, and bearing the sporty features inherited from its Mustang I parent, the 1974 Mustang II (above and left) was an attempt to recapture the flair, excitement, and sales of the original pony car.

Ford's 75th Anniversary

IN 1978, FORD MOTOR Company celebrated its 75th anniversary and the production of its 100 millionth vehicle in the US. From the beginning, Henry Ford's vision had been one of a totally self-sufficient industrial facility. By 1978 Ford's dream had essentially come true. Although the company was still using many outside vendors, its Rouge complex in Dearborn, Michigan, was set up to receive raw materials and process them into the basic industrial products used to make cars.

EVERY MINUTE COUNTED
At Ford's Rouge facility a Mustang rolled off the assembly line every 45 seconds. Above, a body was dropped onto its rear suspension unit.

The Dearborn Assembly Plant (DAP), situated in the midst of this sprawling complex, was home to the Mustang and would be for the life of the carline. Before Mustang, the plant had produced Fairlane models and before that full-size Fords. By 1978 the Rouge facility (named after the nearby Rouge River) had grown into one of the largest industrial complexes in the world, encompassing 1,200 acres and employing more than 28,000 people. Mustangs were rolling off the Rouge assembly line at the rate of one every 45 seconds.

Cars & Culture 1974–78

1974: Car of the Year	1974: Energy Crisis	1976: Cobra II
In 1974 *Motor Trend* magazine named the Mustang II its "Car of the Year." The title was awarded based on the car's new standard of fuel economy and value.	After OPEC cut off oil deliveries to the West, lines formed at gas stations nationwide, and a national "energy-saving" speed limit of 55 mph was introduced.	Anticipating the return of public demand for the musclecar style and power, Ford threw its hat into the ring with the Cobra II. While the car had sassy styling, it offered none of the original Cobra's power.

Praise for the Mustang II	*OPEC oil embargo*	*1976 Cobra II*

People Behind the Mustang

LEE IACOCCA

The man behind the original Mustang was also the visionary behind Mustang II. Reacting to the slump in sales brought on by increased competition, the growing size of the Mustang, and energy concerns, Iacocca drove the Ford team toward a reinvention of the car as a sporty vehicle.

Born Lido Anthony Iacocca, the future president of Ford Motor Company grew up on his family's Ford Model T and A rental car lot. From his youth, his dream was to go into the carmaking business. Iacocca did not want to work for just any company; it had to be Ford. He never wavered from his goal. After earning a master's degree in mechanical engineering at Princeton, he went to Ford.

Lee Iacocca with his brainchildren, Mustang II (front) and I (rear).

In 1956 his slogan "$56 a month for a '56 Ford" worked so well nationally that he was credited with selling 72,000 additional cars that year. His career took off, and by age 36 Iacocca was replacing Robert McNamara as Ford vice president and general manager. Although Iacocca is credited as the force behind the Mustang, the original car was truly a team effort. The Mustang II, which debuted in 1974, was just as undeniably Iacocca's baby. His objective: "create a little jewel." Athough the new '74 Mustang did spike sales at a time when all American car manufacturers were suffering, sales ultimately continued their downward trend. Henry Ford II fired Lee Iacocca in 1978, reportedly because of political and personal differences.

1977: New President	1978: CAFE Laws	1978: Trans Am
James Earl Carter was elected as the 39th President of the United States in 1977. His administration was troubled by an energy crisis and the Iranian takeover of that country's US embassy.	In 1978 the first regulatory laws dictating automobile fuel economy would take effect. The Corporate Average Fuel Economy (CAFE) standard set 18 mpg as the minimum acceptable standard.	At a time when small was in and compliance, not performance, was the standard for US carmakers, Pontiac's trend-defying Firebird Trans Am guzzled gas and announced it loudly via the graphics on its hood.

President Jimmy Carter	*The Pinto made mpg a priority*	*1978 Trans Am hood decal*

1974–1978 Concept

"ALL THE 1974 will have to be is one thing; it will have to be a little jewel." This was Lee Iacocca's response to the challenge of boosting Mustang's ailing sales figures. Fit, finish, ride, handling, and interior appointments would need to evoke the image of European craftsmanship. This was a tall order for the Pinto platform, the basis for Mustang II. And there were more challenges facing the designers and engineers. New federal standards mandated that bumpers be able to withstand a five-mph crash without damage. Meanwhile noise, vibration, and harshness (NVH) problems plagued the development of the "Pintostang." Engineer Bob Negstad vastly improved ride quality with a U-shaped subframe dubbed the "toilet seat" that transferred stresses from the front subframe to the entire floor pan. The Sportiva II concept vehicle was displayed at car shows and racetracks in 1973, providing a glimpse of the safety, design, and styling features to come for 1974.

SPORTIVA INTERIOR
The Sportiva featured an eye-popping gold-and-white interior with an alternate design for the instrument panel.

SPORTIVA II

The Sportiva II could have been Ford's answer to a new convertible model for the Mustang II lineup. It featured a targa-style roof bar to give the passengers extra protection in the event of a crash and displayed many of the traditional Mustang styling cues incorporated into a lithe, taut package.

WINDSHIELD
The windshield on the Sportiva II was laid back a few degress to make it appear sleeker

MIRRORS
Sport-type mirrors were similar to those found on the previous-generation Mustang

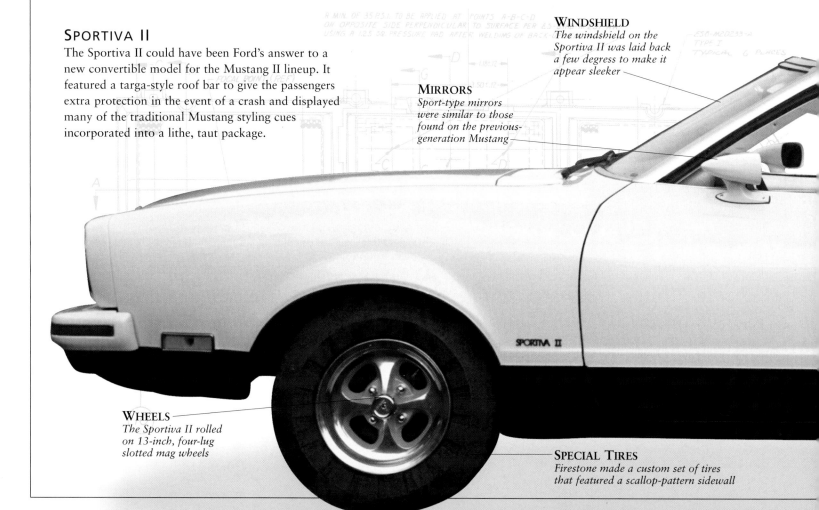

WHEELS
The Sportiva II rolled on 13-inch, four-lug slotted mag wheels

SPECIAL TIRES
Firestone made a custom set of tires that featured a scallop-pattern sidewall

MUSTANG II CONCEPT RENDERINGS

There were several types of design studios at Ford, each of which worked on the car at different stages as it advanced toward production. The designer sketches shown here emanated from what were known as the advanced studios, where designers worked at the purely conceptual level, creating "futuristic" designs intended for possible implementation four to eight years later. Hundreds of these sketches were produced, many of them by young designers from whom the company sought as many fresh, imaginative ideas as possible. Advanced studio designs that were chosen for further implementation moved on to the preproduction studios and then to the production studios, where they were approved by management and ready to be prepared for actual manufacture.

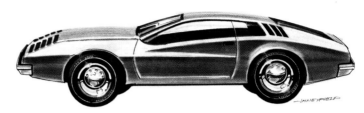

Three sketches from Ford's advanced design studios

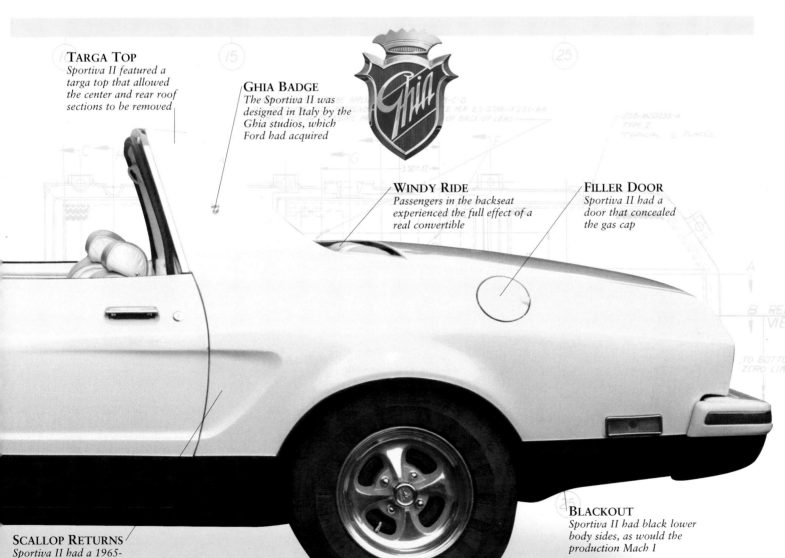

TARGA TOP
Sportiva II featured a targa top that allowed the center and rear roof sections to be removed

GHIA BADGE
The Sportiva II was designed in Italy by the Ghia studios, which Ford had acquired

WINDY RIDE
Passengers in the backseat experienced the full effect of a real convertible

FILLER DOOR
Sportiva II had a door that concealed the gas cap

SCALLOP RETURNS
Sportiva II had a 1965-style side scallop

BLACKOUT
Sportiva II had black lower body sides, as would the production Mach I

1974 Mustang Coupe

1974 SIDE EMBLEM

"THE MOST CHANGED CAR IN THE INDUSTRY!" claimed a Ford advertisement. Mustang IIs of the 1974–78 generation reflected Ford's focus on customer needs. The "sensible size" afforded owners a more personal connection with their vehicles. A new rack-and-pinion steering gear, combined with optional steel-belted radial tires (the era's latest technology), made handling quick and precise. Power from the 171cid (2.8L) V-6, although not neck-snapping, allowed safe entry onto the freeway while producing good fuel economy. The base price of the coupe was more than $3,000; fully optioned it exceeded $4,000, disappointing some buyers. But even as gas shortages intensified Mustang II sales climbed, and the car was deemed a success. Mustang sales hit 385,993 in 1974, nearly triple 1973 sales of 134,867. Even during its worst sales year, Mustang II sold 20,000 units more than during the previous styling period's best year.

THE LITTLE JEWEL
Ford borrowed heavily from the styling cues of the 1965 Mustang to create this reinvention of the car as a sporty machine. It had all the panache of its parent but lacked the power – a sign of the times.

VINYL TOP
The vinyl-covered roof, a popular option, was offered in several colors

SIDE MIRRORS
Dual remote control, color-keyed sport mirrors were sim to those in previous years

TRUNK
Trunk space on the Mustang II shrank by nearly three cubic feet

REAR BUMPER
The Mustang II's rear bumper had a urethane coating that resisted impact and added style

SCALLOP RETURNS
Mustang IIs had a side scallop similar to that of '60s-era Mustangs

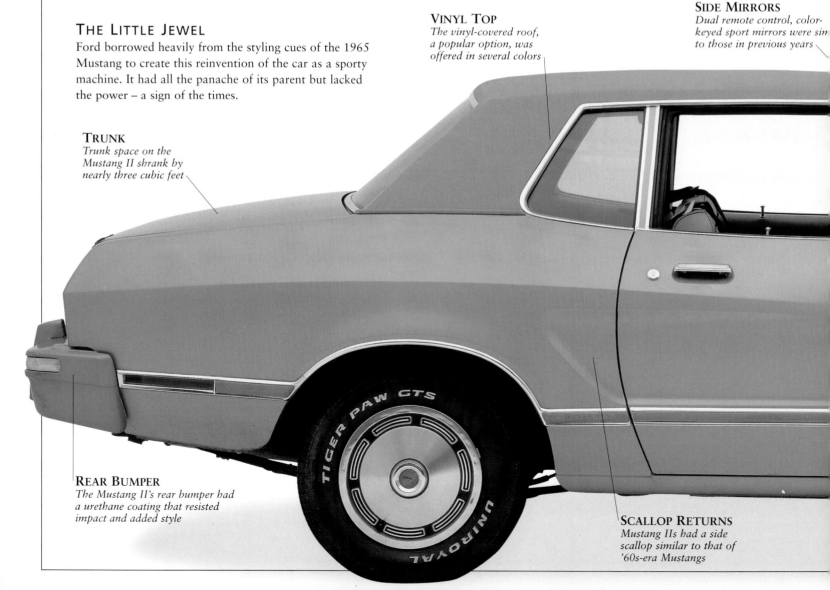

THE 2.3L FOUR-CYLINDER ENGINE

The base 140cid 2.3L four-cylinder engine was not only the first four-cylinder to be offered in a Mustang, but also the first metric American engine. Its design included a cross-flow single overhead cam cylinder head, but it produced only 88 hp, not enough to give zip to a Mustang that weighed almost 3,000 pounds.

The 2.3 engine was the first four-cylinder engine offered with the Mustang

SPECIFICATIONS

MODEL SHOWN	1974 Mustang Coupe
PRODUCTION	177,671
BODY STYLES 1974–78	Coupe, hatchback
CONSTRUCTION	Unibody chassis/body
ENGINES	140cid I-4 (1974–78) 171cid V-6 (1974–78) 302cid V-8 (1975–78)
POWER OUTPUT	88 hp (140cid I-4) to 133 hp (302 cid V-8)
TRANSMISSION	Four-speed manual or three-speed automatic
SUSPENSION	Independent front with coil springs and wishbones; semielliptic leaf springs with Iso-clamps at rear
BRAKES	Manual discs front, drums rear, power assist optional
MAXIMUM SPEED	99 mph (159 km/h) (171cid)
	0–60 mph (0–96 km/h) 13.8 seconds (171cid)
	0–100 mph (0–161 km/h) N/A
	A.F.C. 18.2 mpg (109 hp V-6)

ONE-PIECE FRONT

The Mustang II's front fascia and bumper were molded as one piece. A bumper cover let it pass government regulations.

TAILLIGHTS

Mustang IIs featured larger taillights for safety reasons but continued the modular tri-segment theme.

TIGHT QUARTERS
The space between the front fascia and the fenders had a close tolerance so a gap would go unnoticed

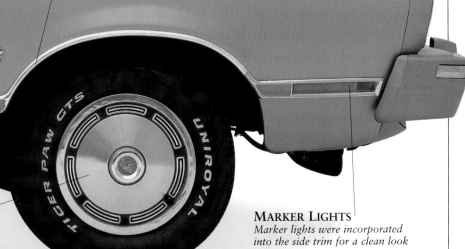

WINDSHIELD
Tinted glass was a common option

BRIGHT TRIM
The wheel openings had chrome moldings

STANDARD WHEELS
This hubcap with red medallion was standard on the coupe

MARKER LIGHTS
Marker lights were incorporated into the side trim for a clean look

1974 Mustang Variations

IN 1974, A CONVERTIBLE BODY STYLE WAS ABSENT from the line for the first time in Mustang history, as was the three-speed manual transmission. Four models were offered based on the two body styles: the standard coupe and hatchback, a Ghia coupe, and the Mach I hatchback. The Mach I continued to be considered the "performance" model even though its standard 2.8L engine did not have the horsepower

1974 MUSTANG II GHIA
The luxury version of the Mustang II was now named the Ghia, after the Italian design studio.

available in previous years. Despite this lack of power, the Mustang II of 1974 was voted *Motor Trend* magazine's "Car of the Year." Its blend of "highway cruiser and suburban economy car," plus its timing in the marketplace – in the midst of the oil crisis – were the features that won Mustang II the coveted title.

DOOR HANDLES
Mustang II received a new pull-up door handle

TIRES
Raised white-letter tires were standard on the Mach I

1974 MACH I
This was the performance model available in 1974, but performance applied to looks only. The Mach I's V-6 engine was not powerful enough at 105 hp to provide real zip.

MACH MARKINGS
Mach I side markings were similar to those on 1971–73 models

BETTER VISION
With much larger glass area, the three-door hatchback offered major improvements in visibility over the previous styling period.

TU-TONE
Mach I featured black paint on the taillight panel and lower body sides

FILL 'ER UP
Gas caps moved from the center of the taillight panel to the driver's side quarter panel

KEY FEATURES
1974 Mustang Mach I

- **Production:** 44,046 units
- 2.8L engine standard
- Black painted lower body side
- Styled steel wheels standard
- Only available in three-door hatchback

WHEELS
Mach I buyers had an option to order forged aluminum wheels for an extra $71

LIGHTS
The tri-segment taillights contained turn signals and backup lights

EXHAUST
Dual tail pipes added a performance look

THE 2.8L, MUSTANG'S FIRST V-6

The first Mustang V-6 was a German-built 171cid 2.8L engine rated at 105 hp. The V-6 was standard in the Mach I for 1974 and optional in other models. The problem with this engine was actually a problem with the car: Mustangs had gotten heavier to meet new car-safety standards. Thus the V-6 did not come close to matching Mustang I performance.

STANDARD V-6
The 2.8L V-6 engine was standard on the Mach I

JUST A TROT
Mustang II's front emblem horse was positioned in more of a trot than the gallop of previous years

GRILLE
1974 would be the only year Mach I would have a chrome grille

TURN SIGNALS
Mounted in the grille, turn signals looked similar to sporty fog lamps

The German-built 2.8L engine had more power than the standard four-cylinder, but still not enough

1975–1976 Mustang

THE MOST CHANGED CAR IN THE INDUSTRY for 1974 was possibly the least changed car in 1975. A 302cid V-8 engine returned to the lineup, ignited by a solid-state electronic ignition system. Rated at 140 hp, it was not a powerhouse like the engines of just five years earlier. The car had an automatic transmission with mandatory power steering and brakes. Dry-pavement handling was improved, but a front-end weight bias, especially on icy roads, could make driving an adventure. Steel-belted radial tires became standard on all models, and the Ghia received a restyled half-vinyl roof, with a rectangular "opera window." The year 1976 would see hardly any changes, with the exception of dubbing the four-cylinder cars as MPG models (emphasizing their fuel economy), an optional manual four-speed transmission for the 302 V-8, and a new appearance package called the "Stallion Group."

KEY FEATURES

1975 Mustang II Ghia

- **Production:** 52,320 units
- **5.0L V-8 engine optional**
- **Restyled quarter windows**
- **Larger grille opening with new design**
- **Radial tires replaced bias-ply as standard tires**

1975 MUSTANG II GHIA

Ghia versions of the Mustang II for 1975 featuring quarter-window trim gave the car a more formal look. Purists did not approve because it hindered rear visibility. Most of the changes made were to the interior, with plush velour cloth and luxurious cut-pile carpeting becoming standard.

STRIPES
Pinstripes were standard on the Mustang II Ghia

V-8 BADGE
This small badge denoted a V-8 under the hood

CHROME STRIPS
1975 would be the last year for chrome trim inset into the bumpers

MUSTANG II SUSPENSION

In the pursuit of a smooth ride, Ford engineers applied new technology to the suspension. In the front suspension, the area where the engine was mounted was isolated by rubber bushings from the main frame of the car. This subframe absorbed much of the vibrations from the engine. At the back of the car, Iso-Clamps allowed the rear suspension to have the same smooth operation as the front. These diagrams show the features incorporated into the Mustang II.

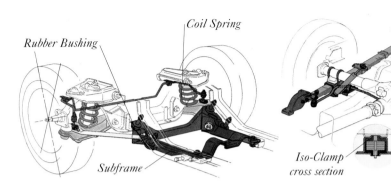

FRONT SUSPENSION *The front subframe was isolated by rubber bushings to reduce vibrations coming from the engine.*

REAR SUSPENSION *Rubber Iso-Clamps allowed smooth movement between the rear axle and leaf springs.*

1976 MUSTANG II STALLION

New for 1976 was the Stallion Group. Essentially this was a Mach I–type appearance package with a special Stallion logo on the front fender. It was available on both the coupe and hatchback.

"OPERA WINDOW"
The quarter window was redesigned for 1975

HALF TOP
Mustang II Ghias had a half-vinyl top

LOGO
With the Stallion Group, this logo appeared on the fender

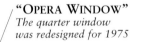

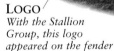

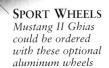

SPORT WHEELS
Mustang II Ghias could be ordered with these optional aluminum wheels

NEW COLOR
Pastel Blue was a popular new color for 1975

1976 DASHBOARD

Interiors did not change much for 1975–76. Mach I had aluminum dash appliqués and a wood-grain shift knob. Gauges were placed directly in front of the driver, and a two-spoke steering wheel was standard. A stylish, leather-wrapped three-spoke wheel was optional.

1977–1978 Mustang

BY 1977, IN SPITE OF GOVERNMENT REGULATIONS and an energy-conscious cultural environment, demand for more performance-oriented cars was starting to rumble once again among the buying public. On the Mustang II Ford responded primarily with cosmetic changes designed to make the car look more fun. Bright colors abounded. A set of removable roof panels over the front seats, dubbed the "T-roof," afforded buyers some open-air fun without the loss of torsional stiffness inherent with a true convertible top. Powertrains carried over from the previous model year, with a six-hp decrease from the 1976 302 engine. The major change for 1978 was the division of the rear seat cushion, which had been a single cushion in previous years.

> **KEY FEATURES**
> **1977 Mustang Mach I T-Roof**
>
> • **Production:** 6,719 units
> • T-roof option added
> • Styled steel wheels standard
> • Front spoiler optional on Mach I
> • Four-way adjustable front seats added

1977 MUSTANG MACH I T-ROOF
Ford originated the idea of a convertible that was not a convertible with this removable roof-panel model. The T-roof provided the driving fun the public had been missing with more safety than a convertible.

WEATHERPROOFING
A rubber gasket lined the inner rim of the T-roof frame, providing a tight seal against the weather

REVISED GRILLE
This grille featured more pronounced horizontal bars

EVEN LESS POWER
Due to new emissions standards, the 302's hp rating dropped from 140 to 134

FRONT SPOILER
Mach I buyers could order this sporty new front spoiler

1978 MUSTANG COUPE

A fashion accessory package offered only on coupes consisted of "Fresno cloth" seat inserts, illuminated driver visor vanity mirror, pockets in the door panels, and other fashion features thought to appeal to female buyers.

NEW COLOR
Tangerine was one of seven new colors for 1978

WIRE WHEELS
First seen in 1977, these hubcaps were included with the fashion accessory package

PINSTRIPES
The fashion accessory package included these sporty pinstripes

EXTRA PROTECTION
All T-roofs incorporated this extra structural bar to keep the car rigid

SIDE WINDOWS
T-roof cars had a smaller quarter window, sacrificing some rear visiblity

NEW SEATS
Mustang IIs of 1977 received a new set of front seats that could adjust four ways

STYLED WHEELS
Once optional, styled steel wheels became standard on all hatchbacks for 1977

THE OPEN AIR T-ROOF

By 1977, the government had imposed such strict safety regulations on cars that the convertible had been completely eliminated from all American auto manufacturers' lineups. People still wanted an open-car feel, and Ford's answer was the T-roof. Making its debut for the 1977 model year, the T-roof had two glass panels that lifted out to give occupants the sensation of the open air. An extra safety loop was incorporated at the rear of the roof to help keep the car rigid. At a retail price of nearly $600, the T-roof option was almost the most expensive option on the list, but if buyers wanted the wind in their hair it was the only way to go.

The 1977 T-roof offered a convertible feel

1976–1978 Mustang Cobra II

COBRA II SNAKE
EMBLEM

WHEN IT CAME TO OFFERING a power-hungry public new options in the late 1970s, the big story at Ford was the new Cobra II. Updating the Shelby look from the previous decade, the Cobra II had stripes, spoilers, a hood scoop, and quarter-window louvers, as well as the optional V-8 powertrain pulled from the non-Cobras. The '76 emulated the GT350, but the comparison stopped on the surface; the flashy '76 Cobra II's standard engine was only a V-6. Still it sold well, more than four times Ford's original sales projection of 5,000. For the 1978 model year, Ford rolled out the King Cobra. Featuring a unique hood decal, special wheels, and a larger front air dam, this was also the first Mustang to feature the "5.0" moniker, which would become legendary by the end of the next decade.

> ### KEY FEATURES
> #### 1978 Mustang King Cobra
>
> - **Production:** 4,318 units
> - **Wild hood graphics**
> - **Standard "Lacy Spoke" wheels**
> - **Big front and rear spoilers**
> - **First use of "5.0" designation**

1978 MUSTANG KING COBRA

With flares, spoilers, and graphics, the King Cobra could be considered the ultimate "macho" Mustang of the day. But an option price of more than $1,200 drove final sticker price over $7,000 – more than most wanted to pay for a Mustang II.

T-ROOF
A T-roof cost an extra $647 on a King Cobra – $50 less than on a standard model

REAR SPOILER
King Cobras had a large rear spoiler

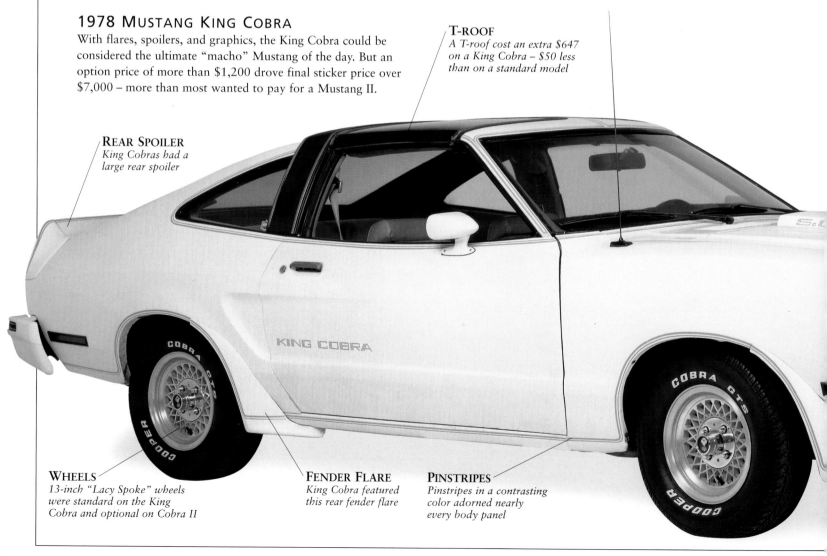

WHEELS
13-inch "Lacy Spoke" wheels were standard on the King Cobra and optional on Cobra II

FENDER FLARE
King Cobra featured this rear fender flare

PINSTRIPES
Pinstripes in a contrasting color adorned nearly every body panel

THE 1976–1977 COBRA II

Considered the most tastefully styled Cobra II, the 1976 model featured Shelby-inspired side stripes, hood scoop, and Cobra emblems. Color choices were white with blue, red, or green stripes, and black with gold stripes.

HOOD SCOOP
This evoked a performance feel, although it was nonfunctional

SNAKE
The same emblem was featured on the 1969 Shelby

SPOILER
The Cobra II package included this front spoiler

T-ROOF
Cobra II could be ordered with a T-roof by 1977

WINDOW LOUVERS
Cobra II used louvers over the rear quarter windows

GRAPHICS
These were modeled after the GT350's, just a little wider to accommodate the Cobra II moniker

WHEELS
The styled steel wheels often found on the Mach I were standard; an optional aluminum wheel was available

HOOD GRAPHICS
Perhaps the raciest thing about the King Cobra was its flaming hood decal

BLACK EYES
Blacked-out headlight bezels made for a sinister look

AIR DAM
King Cobra had an oversized front air dam molded into the front fender flare

COBRA II: OUT IN A BLAZE OF GRAPHICS

Ford changed the Cobra II graphics in late 1977. Many Mustang enthusiasts gawked at the gaudy tricolor stripes with the large "Cobra" running down the body sides. But the 1978 model year would be the last for Mustang II, and Ford wanted to go out with a bang. White painted "Lacy Spoke" aluminum wheels with dual red pinstripes were optional, and the rear window louvers were black. Color choices were white with red, green, or blue racing stripes, and black with gold stripes. The standard engine was the 2.3L four-cylinder, but most buyers went with the 2.8L V-6 or 5.0L V-8. Inside, the Cobra II featured aluminum appliqués on the instrument panel and door panels, low-back bucket seats, and a sport steering wheel. In spite of its critics, the swan-song Cobra II performed and sold well.

The 1978 Cobra II had possibly the loudest graphics of any Mustang

1974–1978 Memorabilia

FORD'S PROMOTIONAL MERCHANDISE machine took off like never before in support of its new baby, the Mustang II. Dozens of items were created to fit into the "active lifestyle" of the Mustang II owner. Many of these were marketed directly to consumers via catalogs or through dealerships. The following quote appeared in the Marvelous Mustang II Merchandise Mart catalog: "This catalog was especially created for you – the Mustang owner – a free-spirited, out-door type, devoted to the 'Mustang way of life'!" The catalog offered Mustang golf clubs, camping equipment, tennis racquets, sportswear, luggage, bicycles, and even sailboats bearing the Mustang II emblem. Other memorabilia from the early 1970s included the usual roster of dealer brochures and promotional materials, many of which remain more valuable than some of the earlier years' editions because they have yet to go into reproduction.

MUSTANG II CUFFLINKS
These cufflinks would make a Mustang statement at any social gathering.

COBRA II GOLF CLUBS
The Mustang II was smaller than previous models, but it still had enough trunk space for a set of golf clubs. These Cobra II golf clubs and bag bearing the Cobra insignia allowed the enthusiast to show his Mustang loyalty on the golf course or in the pro shop.

MODEL CAR KITS AND PROMOS

Despite a loss of interest in plastic models in the middle to late '70s, AMT and MPC both produced 1:25 scale kits of Mustang II hatchbacks. Following on the heels of these kits, dealers offered as promos simplified assembled versions available exclusively at dealerships. The yellow '75 Mach I and red '74 hatchback can bring as much as $65 each from a collector. Interestingly, no coupe versions of the Mustang II were produced in this scale.

DEALER'S SIGN

This dealership sign was designed to replicate the shape of the Mustang II's grille. These were often thrown away after each model year, making them extremely hard to find today. On this particular sign the photo could be swapped out, depending on what car was on sale that week.

A PAPER MACH I

This flyer, available at the dealership, promoted the new '74 Mustang II. It featured a cardboard cutout of a Mach I that could be assembled into a three-dimensional replica of the car.

BROCHURES

The brochures for the Mustang II continue to escalate in value because they are not being reproduced like the brochures of the 1960s. Mint condition examples can bring as much as $50. Odd brochures such as this one for the "Marvelous Mustang II Merchandise Mart" (right) might command an even higher price.

ADS

While ad campaigns for the 1974 Mustang II were more focused on its economical virtues, the focus of 1977 ads had switched to how fun it was to drive a Mustang II.

7

THE THIRD-GENERATION YEARS

1979–1993

The pony car would not only sustain its production volumes for the next 15 years, but also reinvent itself completely – again. This was the era of the Fox platform and the legendary 5.0L engines (left). It was the beginning of a whole new future for Mustang, which kicked off with the release of the 1979 Indy Pace Car (above).

The Birth of the Fox

THE LONGEST CHAPTER in Mustang history opened its pages in 1979. The previous two Mustang designs had dramatically swung from the largest Mustang ever (1971–1973) to the smallest (1974–1978). With gas shortages still weighing heavily on the minds of consumers, Ford laid its chips down on a totally different body design – one with European roots and styling. Ford called the new platform the Fox. The gamble paid off. The Fox seemed to take all the good ideas from previous platforms and make them better. It was lighter and more economical on gas, while retaining power. It was aerodynamically efficient and its performance was precise. Once this new breed of pony car was out of the gate, it roamed American roads for 15 years, the longest of any Mustang in the car's history.

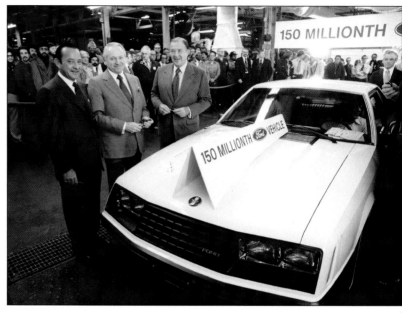

150 MILLION CARS
Ford executives pose with Ford's 150 millionth car, appropriately a 1979 Mustang – the year the company breathed new life into the legendary car.

Cars & Culture 1979–1993

1979: Mustang Pace Car	1980: Reagan Elected	1982: A New Camaro
In 1979, after a 15-year hiatus, the Mustang was again chosen as the official pace car of the Indianapolis 500. In honor of the event, Ford produced 11,000 Indy Pace Car special editions for sale to consumers.	Ronald Reagan was elected President of the United States. During the former actor's eight years in office, carmakers complied with new fuel-economy legislation requiring an average of 27.5 mpg.	Chevrolet kept the competitive heat on Ford by introducing a redesigned Camaro for 1982. That year the new Camaro was chosen to pace the 66th annual Indy 500.

1979 Mustang Indy Pace Car

Ronald Reagan

1982 Camaro Indy Pace Car

People Behind the Mustang

JACK ROUSH

Racing legend Jack Roush's involvement with Ford Motor Company dates back more than 35 years. Born in Covington, Kentucky, in 1942, Roush graduated from Berea College. In 1964, he went to work at Ford in the tooling and assembly divisions. Roush was fascinated by engines and their performance, and he furthered his knowledge with a master's degree in scientific mathematics from Eastern Michigan University. After leaving Ford in 1969, Roush pursued his passion for automotive speed and power and became deeply involved in drag racing. After forming a partnership with driver Wayne Gapp in 1970, Roush won many NHRA, IHRA, and AHRA events in the Pro Stock class. He ended the racing relationship with Gapp in 1976 and formed his own company, Jack Roush Performance Engineering.

Jack Roush, keeping up with lap times

Roush quickly earned a reputation for building fast engines. By 1982 he had formed a partnership with Zakspeed Rennsport of Germany to build Ford race cars. In 1984, Ford hired Roush to oversee the company's IMSA, GTP, and SCCA Trans-Am racing programs. Roush jumped in and responded by winning the manufacturer's title his first year. He has been instrumental in Ford's racing success ever since. Roush Racing has won more than 24 national championships in the two series, including a dozen manufacturer's titles. He has also garnered success in NASCAR Winston Cup racing. His current company, Roush Industries, Inc., employs more than 1,800 people, providing management, engineering, and prototype development services to the motorsports industry.

1984: 20th Anniversary

In 1984, Ford celebrated the 20th anniversary of the Mustang with the release of a 1984½ special edition, featuring a special anniversary color scheme and badges.

1984½ Anniversary GT350

1989: Champs Again

Having abandoned motorsports in 1970, Ford and Mustang returned to the track in the early 1980s. By the late '80s, the Mustang had once again claimed the prestigious Trans-Am title.

1989 Road Atlanta race

1993: Today's Camaro

The year 1993 would see the end of the orignial Fox platform. It would also see an all-new 275 hp Chevy Camaro, sparking a new musclecar war. The Camaro was chosen again to pace the Indy 500.

1993 Camaro Indy Pace Car

1979–1993 Concept

No Ford Mustang differed more radically from its predecessor than the all-new version that appeared in 1979. In fact, this curiously fresh pony car, with its snappy European looks, bore no resemblance to any previous Mustang. The 1979 Mustang was based on a chassis design, dubbed "Fox," that Ford had been developing as part of an attempt to build a "world car" platform on which many cars could be based. The universal platform idea never took off, but the Fox chassis did find its way under the mid-sized Ford Fairmont and, subsequently, the Mustang. Early versions of the Fox-based Mustang showed a squarish body with a jutting front-end section and tightly snipped rear. As further designs were carried out, the new Fox Mustang took on a sleeker European look. Ford produced two show cars, the RSX and IMSA, that pushed the limits of the Fox chassis.

RSX Show Car
Styled by Ghia of Italy, the RSX show car had a distinct European design, with more attention to aerodynamics for both efficiency and looks. This would be the focus for the next generation of Mustangs.

Windshield Wiper
A single wiper was common to many European cars of the day

Scoop
A "power bulge" hood scoop added to the racy appearance of the RSX

Emblem
RSX used the emblem that would appear on 1979–82 Mustangs

Grille Opening
The RSX had a chic forward-slanting, louvered grille

IMSA SHOW CAR

The IMSA show car exhibited racing styling typical of that seen on the race courses of the time. The IMSA was powered by a turbocharged four-cylinder engine.

FLARES
The IMSA had large fender flares to cover the oversized tires

EXHAUST
A large single exhaust tip exited on the left side

TAILLIGHTS
A full-width taillight with "M-U-S-T-A-N-G" was a prominent feature on the rear

GRAPHICS
IMSA stood for International Motor Sports Association

WHEELS
Deep-dish racing-style wheels with clear covers used ultra-wide low-profile tires

HATCHBACK
RSX featured a hatchback similar to the one that would make the production car

WIDE BODY
Blended fender flares allowed for larger tires and looked racy

COUPE CONCEPT

This early styling exercise shows a coupe top with abrupt C-pillars similar to the ones that made it to the production model.

SIDE WINDOW
RSX used a window within a window to allow for passenger ventilation

WHEELS
Custom modular aluminum wheels had a distinctly modern feel

DOORS
RSX's matte black-painted doors gave the car a futuristic look

FURTHER ALONG

This artist's sketch foreshadows many of the features found on the new 1979 Mustang, including the taillights, rear window "slats," and aerodynamic front-end styling.

1979 Mustang Pace Car

INDIANAPOLIS
SPEEDWAY LOGO

THE RADICALLY DIFFERENT new Fox chassis and body design has earned the 1979–93 Mustang classification as the "Third Generation" of the Ford pony car. The 1979 Mustang was introduced in two body styles, a hatchback and coupe. A convertible would not return to the Mustang line until 1983. For the second time since its introduction, the Mustang was named the official pace car of the Indianapolis 500. Ford took advantage of the honor by producing 11,000 Indy Pace Car special editions. The two-tone pewter and black body replicated the paint scheme of the actual pace cars, and a special graphics package was available for dealer   installation. Two engine options were offered for the Indy Pace Car Mustang: a 5.0L V-8 and a turbocharged 2.3L four-cylinder. Other accoutrements to the pace car edition included a special hood and Recaro bucket seats.

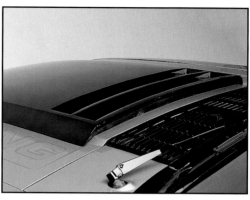

HOOD SCOOP
Indy 500 Pace Car Mustangs received this special reversed hood scoop. Bright orange "Mustang" graphics flanked the scoop sides.

LEADING THE FIELD
Commemorating the 63rd running of the Indianapolis 500 race, this special edition Mustang Pace Car option package was available only in the hatchback body style.

MIRRORS
A new style of side mirror debuted for 1979

COWL
This area was raised, allowing a downward slope of the hood, which improved aerodynamics

GALLOPING MUSTANGS
Three horses ran on the front fenders of the pace car

BELTLINE TRIM
A straight beltline, which also served as a door guard, ran from the front to the rear

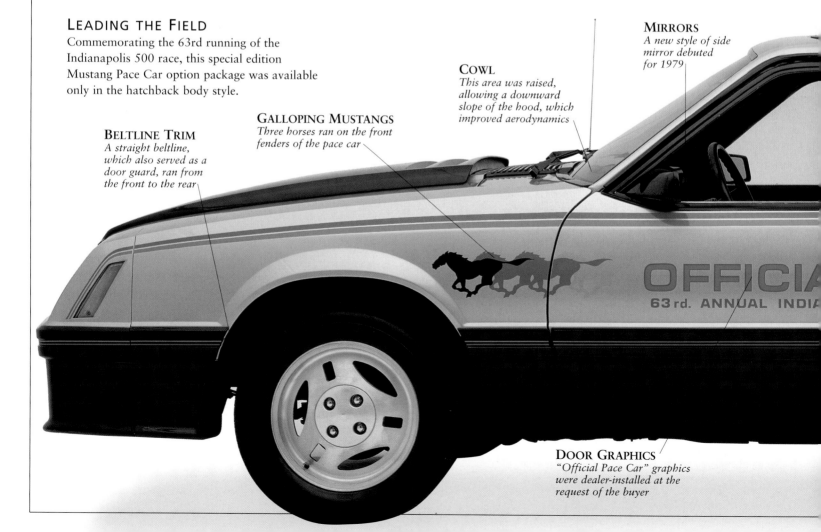

OFFICIA
63rd. ANNUAL INDIA

DOOR GRAPHICS
"Official Pace Car" graphics were dealer-installed at the request of the buyer

THE REAL PACE CAR

The pace cars sold at dealerships were not exactly like the ones pacing the field at Indy. Ford commissioned Jack Roush to modify the real pace car engines with such items as high-performance cylinder heads and a Boss 302 camshaft and crankshaft. The exterior was slightly different and had a T-roof – an option not available on production cars until 1981.

Jackie Stewart taking a lap at Indy

SPECIFICATIONS

MODEL SHOWN	1979 Indy Pace Car Mustang
PRODUCTION	11,000 units
BODY STYLES 1979–93	Coupe and hatchback
CONSTRUCTION	Unibody chassis/body
ENGINES	2.3L I-4 (1979–93) 2.8L V-6 (1979) 3.3L I-6 (1979–82) 3.8L V-6 (1983–86) 4.2L V-8 (1980–82) 5.0L V-8 (1979, 1982–93) 5.0L Cobra (1993)
POWER OUTPUT	88 hp (2.3L I-4) to 235 hp (5.0L Cobra)
TRANSMISSION	Four-speed manual and three- or four-speed automatic
SUSPENSION	Independent McPherson strut front; coil spring, four-link rear
BRAKES	Drums standard; front discs and power assist optional
MAXIMUM SPEED	130 mph (161 km/h) (5.0L) 0–60 mph (0–96 km/h) 6.5 seconds (5.0L) 0–100 mph (0–161 km/h) 17 seconds (5.0L) A.F.C. 18 mpg (5.0L)

FRONT VIEW
Quad headlight buckets were set into the front end. Pace cars also had a special front air dam with fog lamps.

REAR STYLING
The rear taillight panel had a European flair. The pace car featured dual exhaust tips exiting from the left side.

THIRD DOOR
The "hatchback" is actually a fastback roof that opens for interior access

SPOILER
Pace cars had this special rear spoiler

STRETCH JOB
The wheelbase increased to 100.4 inches, more than 4 inches longer than the 1978 Mustang

WHEELS
Pace cars were equipped with the new TRX metric wheel-and-tire combination

1979–1982 Mustang Variations

FIRST-YEAR SALES OF THE THIRD-GENERATION Mustang were extremely encouraging. Total sales for the year, at 369,936 units, exceeded those of the 1978 Mustang II by more than 157,000. Perhaps because of this success, Ford made very few changes to the Mustang during the period 1979–82. 1981 would mark the first year in Mustang history that hatchback models outsold coupes. The trend continued through the end of the Mustang's third generation in 1993. Besides the Mustang Indy 500 Pace Car, the company produced only one special model of note, the Mustang Cobra, which was made from 1979 through 1981. These special Mustangs were available with either V-8 power or the turbocharged 2.3L four-cylinder engine, a $542 option at the time. The turbocharger added 44 hp to the stock 2.3L engine, boosting it to 132 hp. These Cobras are important because they foreshadowed another performance-oriented Mustang of note, the 1984–86 SVO.

1982 MUSTANG COUPE
After being edged out in sales in '81, the coupe in '82 sold fewer units than its hatchback sibling for the second year in a row, this time by about 20,000.

1979 MUSTANG COBRA
The Cobra model was carried over from the Mustang II. It would be the Mustang performance leader in 1979–81.

HOOD SCOOP
A front-opening simulated hood scoop added to the Cobra's racy looks

AERODYNAMICS
The nose of the car was slanted back to reduce the drag coefficient to 0.44, Mustang's lowest ever

GRILLE
1979 Mustangs featured an egg-crate-style grille

1980 MUSTANG COBRA

The 1980 Cobra featured a slightly more subdued graphic scheme than its predecessor, although it was still a bit garish by today's standards.

TURBO
Turbocharged models for 1980 could be identified by this badge

HOOD GRAPHIC
1980 Cobras used a similar graphic to those used on the King Cobra of 1978

SLIGHT CHANGE
The Cobra's grille was based on the 1979 Indy Pace Car; horizontal bars were more pronounced

STRIPING
New stripes graced the side of the Cobra for 1980

SPOILERS
The 1980 Cobra used the front and rear spoilers found on the 1979 Pace Car

---

KEY FEATURES

1979 Mustang Turbo Cobra

- **Production:** 7,000 units (approx.)
- 2.3L turbocharged engine
- Unprecedented aerodynamics
- Available in hatchback only
- First time for metric wheel/tire option

LOUVERS
Rear-window louvers were body color

HATCHBACK
The 1979 Cobra was available only as a three-door model

BLACKOUT
The lower body of the Cobra was painted black

TRX OPTION
Michelin TRX wheels and tires were optional on the 1979 Cobra

MICHELIN TRX SYSTEM

The 1979 Mustang was the first American car that offered the TRX metric wheel-and-tire package. The aluminum wheels were 390x150 mm (15.4x5.9 in). Michelin was called in to design a special tire for the new wheels, because all other cars built in the US were using standard 15-inch-diameter tires. The system did not stop at just the wheels and tires. Ford engineering designed the suspension of the new Mustang to take full advantage of the increased wheel size, offering 1979 Mustang buyers one of the era's best-handling cars on dry pavement.

The TRX wheels featured a modern three-spoke design

1983 Mustang GT

1983 WOULD BE THE YEAR THE MUSTANG returned to performance. The introduction of the 5.0L H.O. (high-output) V-8 engine in 1982 had been met with great joy, but the absence of a four-barrel carburetor meant the car could not take full advantage of the new engine's hardware. In 1983, Ford addressed that need by offering a four-barrel aspirated 5.0L engine that could be further enhanced with a Borg-Warner T-5 five-speed manual transmission. These improvements elevated the Mustang to competitive status among its peers, particularly its archrival, the Chevrolet Camaro. The GT model was the optimum Mustang performer for 1983. A GT Turbo model with a 2.3L turbocharged four-cylinder was also offered mid-year. Ford was returning to its "Total Performance" roots, as evident in the Mustang GT.

> ### KEY FEATURES
> #### 1983 Mustang GT
>
> - **Production:** 27,649 units
> - **5.0L V-8 with four-barrel carburetor**
> - **Five-speed manual transmission optional**
> - **First year for the 5.0 badge**
> - **Larger tires for better handling**

PERFORMANCE RETURNS
For the first time, third-generation Mustang owners had a true high-performance Mustang. The V-8-powered GT was the choice of those who wanted a street contender for the likes of the Chevrolet Camaro and Pontiac Firebird.

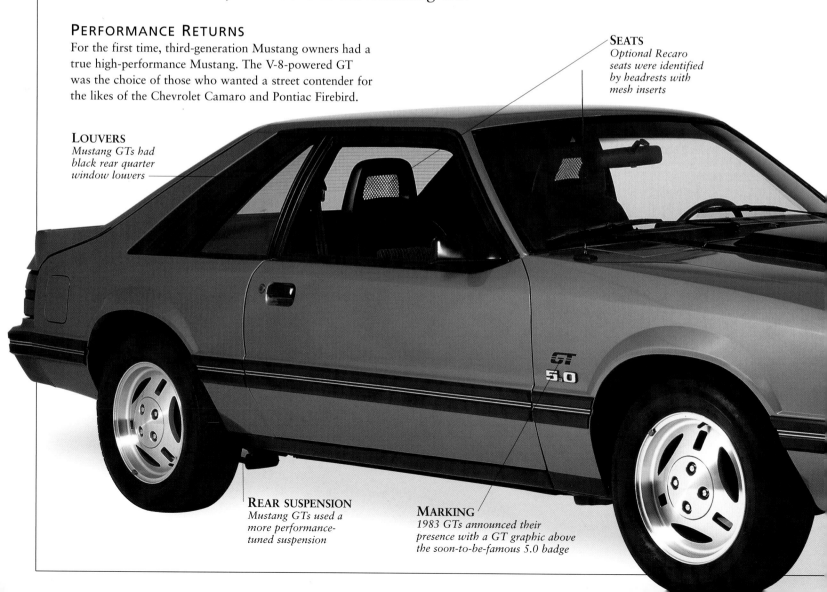

SEATS
Optional Recaro seats were identified by headrests with mesh inserts

LOUVERS
Mustang GTs had black rear quarter window louvers

REAR SUSPENSION
Mustang GTs used a more performance-tuned suspension

MARKING
1983 GTs announced their presence with a GT graphic above the soon-to-be-famous 5.0 badge

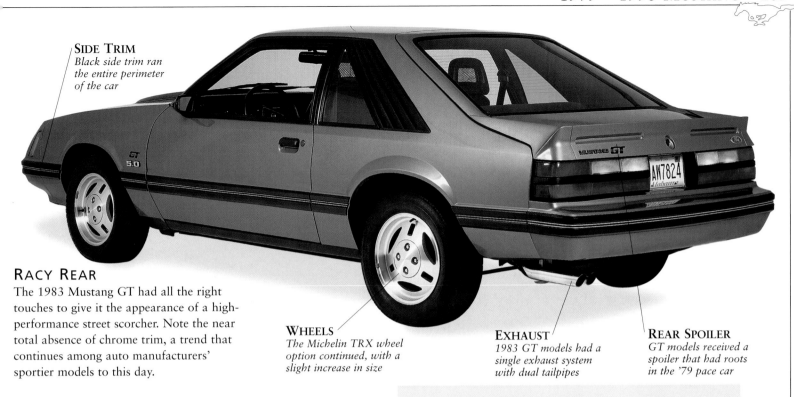

SIDE TRIM
Black side trim ran the entire perimeter of the car

RACY REAR

The 1983 Mustang GT had all the right touches to give it the appearance of a high-performance street scorcher. Note the near total absence of chrome trim, a trend that continues among auto manufacturers' sportier models to this day.

WHEELS
The Michelin TRX wheel option continued, with a slight increase in size

EXHAUST
1983 GT models had a single exhaust system with dual tailpipes

REAR SPOILER
GT models received a spoiler that had roots in the '79 pace car

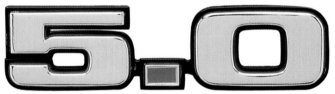

FIVE POINT OH

1983 was the first year that the "5.0" badge appeared. It would be the obvious marker on the front fender of performance Mustangs for the next ten years.

5.0L POWER SURGE

Ford returned the 302cid engine in 1982, a welcome move that boosted horsepower from 120 in 1981 to a 157 rating. The 5.0L H.O. engine did not achieve greatness until 1983, when Ford added the Holley 600cfm four-barrel carburetor. The Holley carb added much-needed air flow, elevating the 5.0L's horsepower to a 175 rating and producing 245 lbs/ft. of torque at 2,400 rpm. The new carburetion system was proudly announced by a classy-looking stamped-aluminum air cleaner featuring labeling that read "5.0 Liter 4V H.O." Even more important, enthusiasts now could purchase their favorite car with a powerplant worthy of the Mustang's sports car heritage.

SCOOP
A reversed scoop was standard on GT hoods

BLACKOUT
The blacked-out hood had roots in such models as the Mach I and Boss

NEW SNOUT
The face of the GT took on a racier look

The 5.0L 4V H.O. (high-output) engine

1983–1986 Mustang Variations

1983 FORD "BLUE OVAL"

1983 SAW A REFRESHING ADDITION to the Mustang stable: A convertible returned to the lineup following a ten-year absence. For this model year, Ford outsourced the conversion of convertibles. The work was done by Cars & Concepts, which received coupes from the Dearborn Assembly Plant and returned them as convertibles. Ford brought convertible-body production into its Dearborn facility a year later. 1984 was also the first year the Mustang SVO hit the streets. In 1985, the Mustang received mild cosmetic surgery in the form of a cleaner front fascia. The egg-crate front grille was replaced by a nose that more closely resembled the clean look of the Mustang SVO. In 1986 Ford added a fuel-injection system and a set of tube exhaust headers, which in later years would make the engine more efficient.

1986 MUSTANG COUPE
On the outside it looked much like the 1979 coupe, but on the inside it had a radically new fuel-injection system.

1983 CONVERTIBLE
Convertible lovers welcomed an all-new, drop-top version of the Mustang in 1983, especially since it could be powered by a 5.0L four-barrel V-8.

INTERIOR
Convertible interiors were available in eight colors, including this red

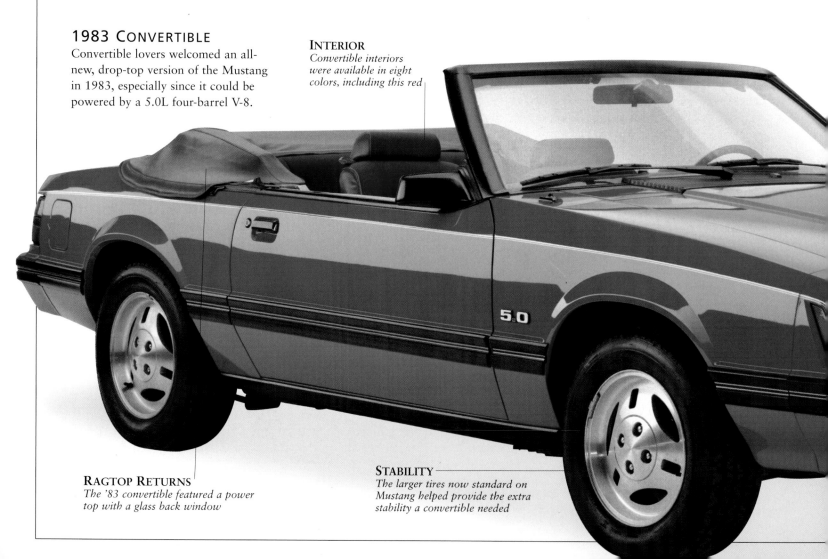

RAGTOP RETURNS
The '83 convertible featured a power top with a glass back window

STABILITY
The larger tires now standard on Mustang helped provide the extra stability a convertible needed

OUTSOURCED
Ford went to Cars & Concepts in Brighton, MI, for conversion from coupes to convertibles.

FRAME
Windshield frame was free-standing, giving a clean look

NEW LIGHTS
Ford revised the taillights for 1983

1984 DASHBOARD
The dashboard had not changed much since its inception in 1979. A curvy three-spoke steering wheel was standard on the GT.

KEY FEATURES
1983 Mustang Convertible

- **Production:** 23,438 units
- **First convertible in ten years**
- **First Fox-based convertible**
- **Available as LX V-6, LX V-8, or GT V-8**
- **Available in 14 colors**

THE TWENTIETH ANNIVERSARY

The big news for 1984 was a special 20th Anniversary Edition Mustang. Considered an '84½, this car was available as either a hatchback or convertible, and buyers could opt for either the turbocharged four-cylinder or the 5.0 H.O. All were painted Oxford White with a Canyon Red interior, and sported original pony-and-stripes side emblems and two special 20th anniversary badges on the dashboard. Ford capitalized on the Mustang's past performance by adding tape side stripes with "GT350" markings, an obvious reference to the Shelby days. Carroll Shelby did not approve of the package, since he had sold the rights to the "Cobra" name but not the "GT350" or "GT500" names. Ford agreed not to use the name again, but only after the first 5,260 cars were built.

POWER
Under the hood, the standard engine for 1983 was the 2.3L, four-cylinder

HOOD
Non-GT cars sported a clean hood

EMBLEM
1983 would be the first year that the Ford "Blue Oval" would grace a Mustang

The 1984½ Anniversary Edition "GT350"

1986 Mustang SVO

SVO FENDER EMBLEM

1986 WAS A TRANSITIONAL YEAR for the Ford Mustang, and the last year of the third generation's initial body style. This would also be the final year of production for Ford's European performance entree, the Mustang SVO. Ford's Special Vehicle Operations (SVO) division had created the car to compete with small European sports coupes such as the BMW 318 and Volkswagen GTI, which were gaining popularity in the United States. The SVO team incorporated performance features never before seen in a production Mustang, such as a turbocharged four-cylinder engine capable of producing more than 200 hp. The SVO also featured suspension alterations that immensely improved handling and body modifications and gave the car the look of a smooth Euro-racer. The Mustang SVO never sold in great numbers due in large part to its price tag, which was approximately $2,500 more than a nicely equipped 5.0L GT. However, the SVO did advance Mustang styling with its fresher, smoother, aerodynamic look.

> **KEY FEATURES**
> ### 1986 Mustang SVO
>
> - **Production:** 3,314 units
> - **Turbocharged four-cylinder engine**
> - **Produced more than 200 hp**
> - **Featured Euro-styling to compete with imported cars**
> - **Special aerodynamic wheels**

A GLIMPSE INTO THE FUTURE
The SVO, produced for just three years, brought new ideas to the Mustang line. Only 9,844 were produced during the period, making this car one of the more collectible of the third-generation Mustangs.

SUNROOF
An SVO buyer could choose the optional sunroof for an extra $355

SCOOP
The SVO's turbocharged engine took in fresh air from this hood scoop

SMOOTH FRONT
The SVO's grille-less nose influenced future Mustangs

HEADLIGHTS
Fully aerodynamic headlights replaced the awkward vertical ones used on earlier SVOs

FOG LAMPS
Fog lamps were inset into the smooth lower front valance panel

SMOOTH STYLING

The SVO received many body modifications that separated it from other Mustangs. Much emphasis was placed on giving the car a clean, European look.

SPOILER
The single-wing spoiler became a free option on the '85½ and '86 SVO

SUSPENSION
SVO used Koni shocks at all four corners to improve cornering

SVO STYLING
One clean slat replaced the louvers found on standard Mustangs

EXHAUST
The dual exhaust not only looked good but also improved performance

HIGH LIGHT
1986 marked the first year for the center high-mounted stoplight (CHMSL)

AERO WHEEL

Special 16-inch aerodynamic slotted wheels were available only on the SVO. The only other American production car at the time that had wheels this size was Chevrolet's Corvette.

SVO TURBO FOUR-CYLINDER

The Mustang SVO was available with only one engine: a 2.3L four-cylinder Turbo. Despite its small size, this specially developed powerplant was able to produce 175 hp, a number that increased to 205 hp in late 1985. The fuel-injected 2.3L Turbo was able to achieve such a high horsepower rating as a result of its turbocharger and intercooler, which used exhaust gas to force intake air through the intercooler to the cylinders. The engine was also lightweight, making the Mustang even quicker. Thanks in large part to the 2.3L Turbo, Ford achieved its goal of producing an engine competitive with those being produced for European sports cars. But it never caught on, because it could not undo America's love affair with the V-8.

STRIPES
Pinstripes added a bit of refinement to the body

FLARES
Rear flares were added to counteract the negative impact on aerodynamics caused by oversized rear tires

TIRES
SVO used 225/50-16 Goodyear tires

The 2.3L Turbo engine packed up to 205 hp

1987 Mustang GT

"5.0" FENDER EMBLEM

THE THIRD-GENERATION MUSTANG WENT THROUGH its most dramatic styling changes in 1987. Rumors had been floating around that it would be based on the front-wheel drive Mazda (Probe) platform, but that was not to be. Several styling features were picked up from the 1986 Mustang SVO, including the aerodynamic headlights and smooth front. With the SVO gone, the GTs were featured as the top performance models in 1987, available with either a four- or eight-cylinder engine. GT styling featured an air dam with a set of scoops located just forward of the front wheels to match the side ground effects with a scoop in the rear. The interior of the GT got a nice dose of restyling as well, including an all-new dashboard. Performance fans were delighted to see the 5.0L V-8 get an increase in horsepower with a revised fuel injection body and cylinder heads boosting power to 225 hp.

KEY FEATURES

1987 Mustang GT

- **Production:** 37,088 units
- Heavy restyling resulted in clean look
- "Cheese-grater" taillights
- 12-spoke turbine wheels standard
- Improved fuel injection

CLEAN LOOK
The side louvers were replaced with one clean sheet of glass

A NEW FACE FOR AN OLD FRIEND
After eight years, the third-generation Mustang finally got a facelift in 1987. The Mustang GT received more cosmetic changes than other models.

SCOOPS
Rear side scoops were part of the GT package

NEW WHEELS
Turbine wheels, offered for the first time, were standard on GT

GT STYLING

The GT model came with an extensive ground-effects package, including special rocker panels and valances front and rear.

SPOILER
GT models had a spoiler added to the rear hatch

THE 5.0
1987 Mustang GTs were equipped with the 225 hp 5.0L V-8

LOWER ROCKERS
GT models had ground effects that included a recessed "Mustang GT" logotype

LOWER BELTLINE
1987 models featured lower beltline trim than previous models

REAR VALANCE
The ground effects continued on the rear with "Mustang GT" recessed to match the sides

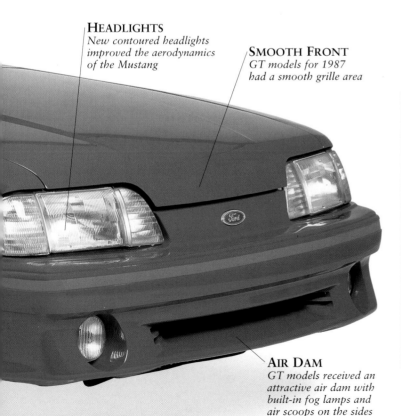

TAILLIGHT

GT models received a louvered taillight treatment often referred to as "cheese-grater" taillights.

HEADLIGHTS
New contoured headlights improved the aerodynamics of the Mustang

SMOOTH FRONT
GT models for 1987 had a smooth grille area

AIR DAM
GT models received an attractive air dam with built-in fog lamps and air scoops on the sides

MORE POWER FOR THE 5.0

In 1986, Ford's 5.0L V-8 received the latest technology in fuel delivery with the debut of a sequential multi-port fuel-injection intake system. This system was much more efficient than the carburetor setup that had been on the Mustang V-8 since its inception. First-year problems with the new fuel-injection technology accounted for a decrease from 210 hp to 200 hp, but by the next year Ford had figured this system out. A new freer-flowing cylinder head and a larger throttle body accounted for a new rating of 225 hp at 4,000 rpm for 1987. Now with over 300 lbs/ft. of torque, the Mustang was starting to gallop again.

The fuel-injected 5.0L H.O.

1987–1991 Mustang Variations

1991 Mustang Aluminum Wheel

BY THE LATE EIGHTIES the Fox-based Mustang had fully matured into a worthy driving machine. Somewhat ironically, Mustang buyers who wanted to get the best performance out of their cars didn't opt for the top-of-the-line Mustang GT fastback or convertible. Many owners for whom speed was a priority chose the LX coupe instead. Although the Mustang coupe was not available as a GT, the car could be had with the same engine and drivetrain in the LX model. The coupe's lighter weight (approximately 200 pounds) and stiffer body made it a faster and more nimble vehicle than an identically equipped fastback model. Interestingly, fastback models far outsold coupes overall during the years of the third-generation Mustang, as opposed to the sales trends of the earlier generations of the car.

1987 HATCHBACK
The hatchback model continued to be the best selling model in the Mustang stable. With optional 5.0 power, it was considered fast and affordable transportation.

1991 MUSTANG LX COUPE
The Mustang coupe is often thought of in automotive terms as a "sleeper," or a car whose performance is hidden by its looks.

FRONT BUMPER
Coupe models were available only with the standard front bumper as opposed to the aerodynamic add-ons of the GT

GRILLE
The LX model had this grille opening unlike its GT sibling

AIR SUPPLY
The engine received most of its fresh air supply through this lower valance opening

5.0 EMBLEM
LXs equipped with the V-8 continued the use of the 5.0 emblem

SPECIAL COLORS
All special edition Mustangs came in Emerald Green with white interiors

LUGGAGE RACK
The special edition could be ordered with a luggage rack on the trunk

1990 SPECIAL EDITION MUSTANG

Mustang celebrated its 25th anniversary with a limited edition of 2,000 special edition cars. Although the anniversary year was technically 1989 $^1/_2$, the limited edition was a 1990 model.

GT WHEELS
Special editions had GT spoked alloy wheels and tires

C-PILLAR
The rear roof pillars are wider than they look; the side window glass covers much of their girth

---

KEY FEATURES

1991 Mustang Coupe

- **Production:** 21,513 units
- **"Sleeper" choice for performance**
- **Stiffer body than other models**
- **Driver's side air bag standard**
- **Optional five-spoke wheels**

A MUSTANG FOR THE LAW

By 1991, a Mustang equipped with a 5.0L engine had returned to the days of the muscle car. Next to a Chevy Corvette or a European exotic car, no other production car could touch a 5.0L Mustang on the streets. Local and state law officers started to see a need for a high-speed pursuit car, and the full-size Chevrolet Caprices and Ford Crown Victorias just didn't have the pep needed to catch something like a 5.0L Mustang. To help remedy this, Ford offered a "Special Service Package" to police departments that included a Mustang coupe outfitted with extra options such as 5.0L engines equipped with heavy-duty engine cooling systems and a calibrated 160 mph speedometer. Police departments ordered nearly 15,000 Mustangs to help catch the bad guys.

The police had a high-speed pursuit car with a 5.0L Mustang

STIFF BODY
The coupe body was stiffer than the other models, a trait that improved handling

FIVE SPOKES
New five-spoke wheels were optional on 5.0L LX models

1991–1993 Mustang Variations

DURING 1991–93, THE MUSTANG EXPERIENCED fewer changes than at any other time in the third generation. Other than the Cobra model of '93 and a few special editions that were really no more than special colors, the Mustang didn't change at all. A new Mustang was on the horizon, but Ford didn't really know when it would be ready, and was reluctant to put much money into changing the already-refined Fox platform. This opened the door for performance engineer Steve Saleen, who has become to modern Mustang fans what Carroll Shelby was during the 1960s. The first Saleen Mustang, produced in 1984, featured aerodynamic body panels and racing suspension components, but the company began adding engine modifications thereafter. By the early '90s, the Saleen had matured into a thoroughbred, endorsed by Ford and available through local dealers.

SALEEN INTERIOR
Flo-fit leather seats with mesh headrest inserts offered optimum comfort.

1991 SALEEN CONVERTIBLE
Loaded with performance and styling touches, the Saleen was the Mustang for the die-hard owner who wanted more than a GT or LX could offer.

INTERIOR
Interior modifications included racing-style seats and an upgraded stereo system

ROLL BAR
Saleen convertibles featured an integral roll bar reminiscent of those found on the late '60s Shelbys

AIR SPOILER
A special rear spoiler was designed by Saleen

SIDE SKIRTS
Custom "aero" side panels were a trademark of Saleen Mustangs

GRAPHICS
Saleen Mustangs had distinctive graphic appliqués

SUSPENSION
Patented "Racecraft" suspension components improved handling

WHEELS
Saleen wheels were identified by their "S" logo center caps

BRIGHT YELLOW
Only 1,419 convertibles were produced in this color.

BRIGHT RED
This 1992½ limited edition would be hard to miss with its bright red paint

1992–93 LIMITED EDITIONS

To help sagging sales, Ford offered a couple of "Limited Edition" Mustangs. Considered a 1992½, a Vibrant Red convertible was available with white wheels and interior, and a special rear spoiler. Only 3,333 were produced for 1992½. A similar package returned for 1993 with yellow as the color of choice.

DASHING DASH

Mustang GT and 5.0 LX models had 140 mph speedometers by 1991, all others used the standard 85 mph speedometers.

KEY FEATURES

1991 Saleen Mustang

- **Production:** 92 units (30 convertibles)
- **Designed by Steve Saleen**, race driver and performance engineer
- **5.0L EFI H.O. engine**
- **Styling touches reminiscent of Shelby**
- **"S" logo on wheels**

1993 SVT COBRA

In an effort to boost Mustang's performance image for the upcoming years, Ford formed the Special Vehicle Team (SVT). Like its SVO (Special Vehicle Operations) predecessor, SVT was challenged to create special edition Mustangs with enhanced engine and chassis components. The first effort for the team was the 1993 SVT Cobra. They started by reconfiguring the engine with larger intake manifolds and exhaust ports, allowing the engine to breathe more easily. These, along with other modifications, boosted the SVT Cobra's horsepower rating to 235. The chassis received a host of modifications that gave it a lower stance and allowed it to handle more like a true sports car. Larger 17-inch alloy wheels with wider, speed-rated Goodyear tires were mounted all around, and extra stopping power was provided by disc brakes with vented rotors on all four corners.

UNDER THE HOOD
Internal engine modifications gave the Saleen a bit more power

AIR DAM
Although similar to the one found on the GT, the Saleen's was more aggressive

The 1993 SVT Cobra was offered only in red, black, or teal

Back to the Track

FORD RETURNED TO RACING in the early 1980s after abandoning motorsports altogether in 1970. The company got its feet wet by hiring the German company Zakspeed, which had entered into a partnership with racing specialist Jack Roush, to build IMSA GTP (Grand Touring Prototype) Mercury Capri and Ford Mustang race cars. These early GTP cars had moderate success, but it wasn't until 1984, when Ford hired Roush to head up their IMSA and Trans-Am programs, that the company finally struck gold. Roush, along with Mustang SVO chassis specialist Bob Riley, brought Ford back to the forefront of racing by building highly competitive race cars and hiring top drivers to pilot them. In two seasons alone, 1985–86, Roush-built cars won 17 of 34 races on the Trans-Am circuit. During the period of 1984–89 Roush-built Mustangs collected 46 Trans-Am wins – more victories than all other manufacturers combined – a clear signal that the Mustang was back!

QUICK PIT
The pit crew of teammates Scott Pruitt and Bruce Jenner change tires in the 1986 IMSA event at Watkins Glen.

1989 ROAD ATLANTA
Dorsey Schroeder barrels though a turn at Road Atlanta, on his way to the event win and Mustangs first Trans-Am championship since Parnelli Jones did it in 1970.

WINNING MUSTANG DRIVERS

During the 1980s, Ford's driver list included some of the most successful on the circuit. Tom Gloy was the first to bring the Mustang back to victory lane by winning the Trans-Am event at Sears Point Raceway in 1981. Gloy brought Lyn St. James onto his team in 1983 to go up against their Camaro archrivals. St. James had made racing history in '79 by finishing second at Road Atlanta – the highest finish ever for a woman in an American professional road race. The Mustang peaked in 1989, its 25th anniversary year, with Dorsey Schroeder behind the wheel of a red, white, and blue Mustang bearing the number 25. His Jack Roush-prepared car won half of the 14 Trans-Am races that year going on to win the first Trans-Am title for Mustangs in nearly 30 years. He would continue to win with Mustangs for the next several years etching his name among the ranks of Mustang racing greats.

Tom Gloy was the first to get a Mustang back in victory lane late in 1981. His 7-Eleven-sponsored cars won three races in 1984

Dorsey Schroeder dominated the 1989 Trans-Am series with seven wins and 12 top-five finishes out of the total of 14 races

Lyn St. James is one of the finest female race drivers in the world. She campaigned a Mustang for the '83 season with several top-five finishes

1982 MUSTANG IMSA

The Bill Scott-prepared/SVO-sponsored Mustangs were powered by turbocharged four-cylinders. Although competitive, these cars had it tough racing against Porsches that had twice the horsepower.

1984 MUSTANG GTP

A Mustang in name alone, this front-engined, turbocharged four-cylinder Mustang GTP was driven by 1986 Indianapolis 500 winner Bobby Rahal at Road America near Elkhart Lake, Wisconsin.

1979–1993 Memorabilia

MUSTANG'S THIRD GENERATION LASTED almost as long as all the previous years combined, yet collectibles from this period are not any more abundant than those of previous years. This is most likely due to the fact that the Mustang changed very little from year to year. The new 1979 model kicked off with a bang, however, with Ford taking advantage of the Mustang's Indy 500 Pace Car status. For the children of Mustang aficionados, a go-cart replica of the Mustang pace car, powered by a 2.5 hp gas engine, was available through Ford dealerships. The cart's fastback body was treated to the same body colors and graphics of the special edition Indy 500 Pace Car. Mustang model kits abound for this period, with all the major manufacturers having produced kits of the Mustang at various times throughout the 1979–93 period.

APPAREL
Items such as T-shirts, hats, and jackets were marketed very strongly during this time, making them not highly collectible. This commemorative 1979 Indy 500 jacket did spark some interest with collectors.

GO-CART
In the '60s kids had to have pedal cars; by the '80s they wanted engines for their Mustangs. Only 2,000 motorized mini-Mustangs were manufactured by F.W. Associates in Arizona and they were sold as promotional items through Ford dealerships for a retail of $695. They featured fiberglass bodies and "Official Pace Car" graphics replicating those of the 1979 Indy Pace Car.

SPOILER
The car had its own fiberglass spoiler

TRIM
Just like the real car, the smaller version had a black beltline

DOOR GRAPHICS
These matched those on the grown-up version of the car

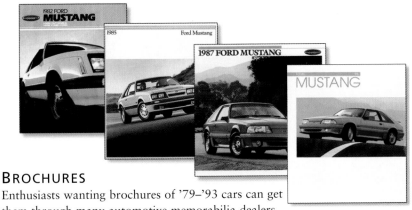

MUSTANG POSTCARDS

Potential buyers often had not decided whether or not they needed a new car. Salesmen would send them one of these postcards to help remind them that their Mustang was still there.

BROCHURES

Enthusiasts wanting brochures of '79–'93 cars can get them through many automotive memorabilia dealers around the country. It is even possible that your local Ford dealership has some of the later editions in stock.

MODEL KITS

By 1979, model kits were becoming quite popular again. Revell/Monogram issued Mustangs in various forms in 1/24 scale. They also offered many of the popular Mustang race cars of the era, including Dorsey Schroeder's 25th Anniversary car of 1989. AMT/MPC continued to produce their own line of Mustangs only theirs were in the more popular 1/25 scale.

CORGI MUSTANG

In 1982 Corgi of England produced a die-cast replica of a Mustang hatchback in approximately 1/43 scale. The hood and rear hatch opened to show off the engine and interior detail. Two versions were offered; the yellow one pictured and one in white with red and blue trim.

HOT WHEELS

Hot Wheels returned with a 1979 Mustang for that year's new line. Offered in many different colors since then, this example is a rare blue variation from Mattel of India.

ADVERTISMENTS

Ads for the convertible were hot for 1984. The ad on the left shows the US Women's Volleyball Team endorsing the Mustang, and the ad on the right features the 20th anniversary model.

8

A NEW MILLENNIUM

1994–2001

1994 marked the much-anticipated debut of Ford's fourth major Mustang redesign. The new pony car had plenty of power and more panache than ever, with styling cues picked up from 1964. It was a modern Mustang lover's dream come true, especially when packaged with the performance and styling options of the SVT Cobra (above and left).

Everything Old Is New

THE REINVENTED MUSTANG FOR 1994 blended classic with cutting edge. Ford chose to continue the rear-wheel-drive platform and front-engine powertrain for another product cycle, knowing how dedicated Mustang fans were to this classic American combination. But almost everything else changed. Only 36 months before the new car's introduction, approval was given to extensively revise the existing Fox platform to increase torsional stiffness and provide a more rigid foundation. Thus a number of structural changes were incorporated into the new Mustang, dubbed

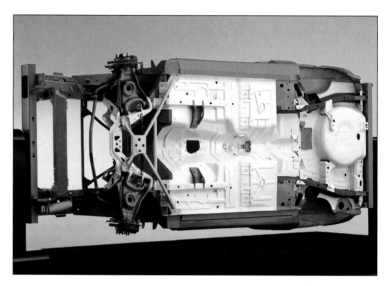

A BETTER DESIGN

Ford redesigned most of the chassis to create more responsive handling and a smoother ride. On this full-scale model the colored parts are all new; only the white has been carried over from '93.

Fox-4, to provide better handling and improve the quality of the manufacturing process. Styling was much bolder and less angular than in previous years, but the traditional pony returned to the center of the grille, and the classic side scoops once again graced the Mustang's flanks. It was a new beginning, with Mustang heritage intact.

Cars & Culture 1994–2001

1994: Indy Pace Car	1996: Pontiac Trans Am	1996: New 4.6L Engine
For the third time in its history, the Mustang was chosen to pace the Indy 500 in 1994. Jack Roush built the real pace cars, and Ford released a limited edition of 1,000 SVT Cobras for consumers.	Although the redesigned Pontiac Trans Am debuted in 1993, it really turned the heat up when the WS-6 option became available for 1996. With 305 hp, "Ram-Air" induction, and a race- tuned suspension, the Mustang would have to eat more oats to keep up.	In 1996, Ford introduced the SVT Cobra 4.6L DOHC engine. With four valves per cylinder and 305 hp, the 4.6L gave the Mustang a level of performance never before available in a popularly priced car.

Third time for Indy pacing	*1996 WS-6 Trans Am*	*4.6L DOHC engine*

People Behind the Mustang

JANINE BAY

Janine Bay joined Ford in 1976 as a product engineer. She worked as both a product design engineer and product planning analyst before being named chief product analyst in Strategy and Advanced Planning in 1987. She worked on the Mustang/Probe small specialty segment strategy and became the Mustang powertrain section supervisor in Car Programs Management in 1989. She was then appointed vehicle planning specialist with responsibility for Strategy and Advanced Planning and Vehicle Engineering. In 1991 she was assigned to create and organize Special Vehicle Engineering and the Special Vehicle Team, which launched the 1993 Ford Mustang Cobra.

Following the Cobra launch, Bay was appointed manager of durability and development analysis with the task of improving the company's high mileage durability. As Ford entered into 2000,

Janine Bay, Mustang Vehicle Line Director, 1994–1999

she led the transition team responsible for defining and organizing Ford's Global Test Operations. In October 1994, she was named Mustang vehicle line director. She was one of the first women to oversee a product line and to manage a sports car division. In this position, Bay led efforts to redefine the value equation for Mustang and launch the 1999 model. Bay now serves as Managing Director of Global Vehicle Personalization. Her many other activities include chairing the Professional Women's Network at Ford and active involvement on the board of Mustang Club of America. With her strong passion for the customer, abililty to build diverse technical teams, and commitment to quality of life issues both inside and outside the workplace, Janine Bay is highly regarded as a technical leader and an agent of change. As such, she has been instrumental in the continuing success of today's Mustang.

1999: 35th Anniversary	1994–2000: Racing	2001: Bullitt Car
In 1999, Ford celebrated the 35th anniversary of the Mustang with a freshening of the fourth-generation body design and an anniversary badge for all 1999 model cars. Cobra models also had new independent rear suspensions.	Ford thundered into victory lane in the 1990s. In 1994, the Roush and Gloy teams helped Ford win the Manufacturers' Cup. Roush driver Tommy Kendall dominated the Trans-Am series in 1997 with 11 wins out of 13 races.	Echoing the legendary style of the 1968 Mustang GT driven by Steve McQueen in the movie "Bullitt," Ford released a special-edition, extra- horsepower Bullitt Mustang GT limited to 6,500 cars in 2001.

1999 Anniversary GT

Tommy Kendall's 1997 Mustang

2001 Bullitt Mustang GT

1994–2001 Concept

IN THE PROCESS OF DEVELOPING the fourth-generation Mustang, the Ford design team considered three proposals nicknamed Bruce Jenner, Arnold Schwarzenegger, and Rambo. Each of them had root elements of the Mustang heritage with visual cues that shouted "Mustang!" The Schwarzenegger proposal, more aggressive than Jenner but more traditional than Rambo, won. In 1992 Ford gave the public a sneak peek at the new car via the Mach III concept car. Like all concept cars, the Mach III appeared more progressive than the production model, but many of its features would translate into the 1994 production Mustang.

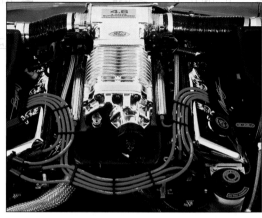

MACH III ENGINE
The Mach III was powered by a 4.6L modular engine topped off with a supercharger. The 4.6L engine would make production by 1996.

MACH III
The Mach III was a teaser for the public just as the two-seat Mustang I had been in 1962. Powered by a supercharged V-8 engine producing 450 hp, it could do 0–60 mph in 4.5 seconds. The long nose, short rear deck, and highly sculpted carbon fiber body were nothing short of sensuous.

SCOOPS
The hood featured intake scoops which would carry over to production cars

WINDSHIELD
The chopped windshield gave the car an ultra-low "speedster" look

MIRRORS
Mach III's molded side mirrors had a sculpted, organic feel

GRILLE
The Mach III grille opening was similar to that of the production car

SIGNAL LIGHTS
The Mach III had its turn signals built into the headlights, as would the production car

THE DESIGN FINALISTS

Beginning in late 1989, Ford was designing the next-generation Mustang. Three clay models were built and given code names to keep the project under tight security. The first design was called "Jenner" after the Olympian-turned-Ford-race-driver. Jenner was not a bad-looking design, but it was deemed not aggressive enough. At the other end of the spectrum was "Rambo." With its racy, even mean-looking design, Rambo was too radical for production. The final car, "Schwarzenegger," had the look that Ford wanted, and the design went on to become the fourth-generation Mustang.

The Jenner proposal was the most conservative of the three

Schwarzenegger was the proposal that won the right to be produced

Rambo was styled to have an aggressive appearance

TWO SEATS
The Mach III had room for only two people

SIDE SCOOP
A large side scoop returned on the Mach III

BIG WHEELS
The car's 19-inch wheels gave it a powerful, racy stance

MACH III INTERIOR

Much like the Mustang I of more than 30 years ago, the Mach III was a two-seater. Many of the design features of the interior made it into production, most notably the twin-pod dashboard.

1994 Mustang Convertible

1994 GT EMBLEM

LIKE ITS FIRST-GENERATION COUSIN, the 1994 convertible was selected as the pace car for the Indy 500. The Mustang convertible, like all 1994 models, was well received by Mustang fans and sold well. The 1994 production Mustang sold a total of 123,198 vehicles, almost 10,000 units more than the previous year. Convertible sales were a healthy 53,714.

Ford offered outstanding new performance options on all 1994 models. A 5.0L V-8 engine was based on the same thin-wall, 260cid cylinder block design from 30 years earlier. V-8 cars had two catalytic converters, balance tube, and two mufflers tuned to rumble. And while the new body was far sleeker than the 1993 car, styling cues pleased Mustang fans with echoes of 1964.

REMOVABLE HARDTOP
An optional lift-off hardtop was offered for convertible models in late 1994. At over $1,000, fewer than 500 of these were ordered.

ANATOMY OF A CONVERTIBLE
This drawing by David Kimble shows the 1994 Mustang from the inside out. At this time Mustang convertibles were being produced at the Dearborn Assembly Plant.

STRUTS
MacPherson-strut front suspension with revised geometry provided good handling on '94 models

PONY RETURNS
The pony returned to the center of the grille after a 16-year absence

1994 INDY PACE CAR

For the third time in its history, the Mustang was chosen to pace the field for the Indy 500. Parnelli Jones would once again pilot the car, this time a Roush-built Cobra setting the pace for the 78th annual race. A Shelby-type roll bar was added to the pace cars to house the flashing light unit. Ford again produced replicas of the car, this time limiting them to 1,000 cars. They were all SVT Cobra models and only came in red. The real pace cars were equipped with automatic transmissions, but the replicas were all five-speed manual. Much as in 1979, the "Official Pace Car" decals were dealer installed.

1994 Mustang Indy pace car built by racing veteran Jack Roush

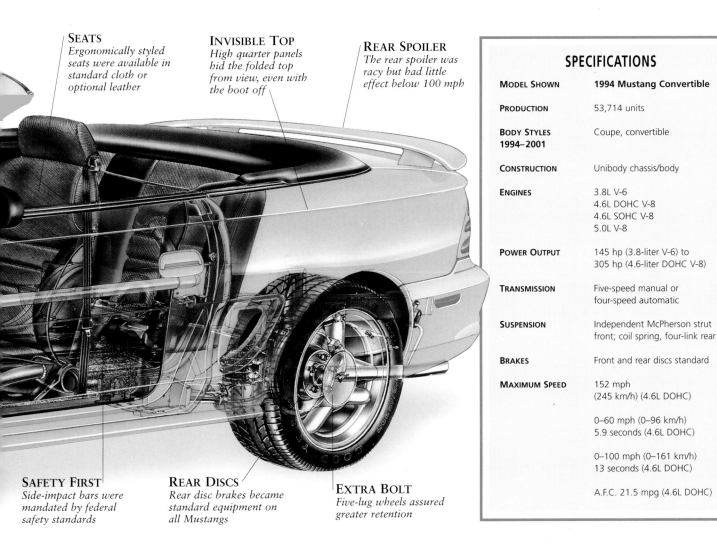

SEATS
Ergonomically styled seats were available in standard cloth or optional leather

INVISIBLE TOP
High quarter panels hid the folded top from view, even with the boot off

REAR SPOILER
The rear spoiler was racy but had little effect below 100 mph

SAFETY FIRST
Side-impact bars were mandated by federal safety standards

REAR DISCS
Rear disc brakes became standard equipment on all Mustangs

EXTRA BOLT
Five-lug wheels assured greater retention

SPECIFICATIONS

MODEL SHOWN	1994 Mustang Convertible
PRODUCTION	53,714 units
BODY STYLES 1994–2001	Coupe, convertible
CONSTRUCTION	Unibody chassis/body
ENGINES	3.8L V-6 4.6L DOHC V-8 4.6L SOHC V-8 5.0L V-8
POWER OUTPUT	145 hp (3.8-liter V-6) to 305 hp (4.6-liter DOHC V-8)
TRANSMISSION	Five-speed manual or four-speed automatic
SUSPENSION	Independent McPherson strut front; coil spring, four-link rear
BRAKES	Front and rear discs standard
MAXIMUM SPEED	152 mph (245 km/h) (4.6L DOHC) 0–60 mph (0–96 km/h) 5.9 seconds (4.6L DOHC) 0–100 mph (0–161 km/h) 13 seconds (4.6L DOHC) A.F.C. 21.5 mpg (4.6L DOHC)

1994–1995 Mustang Variations

MUSTANGS FOR 1995 CARRIED OVER most of the features of the 1994 models. Taillights continued the Mustang three-element design tradition even though many enthusiasts did not approve of their horizontal positioning. Ford continued to move with V-8 power for Mustang, but 1995 would be the last year for the venerable Windsor-produced small block. Absent from the powertrain options for the first time in 20 years was the 2.3L four-cylinder engine. A GTS model was added to the lineup, providing a less expensive V-8 alternative to the pricier GT models. Mustang buyers voted their confidence, making the 1995 models one of the decade's best sellers, with 185,000 units sold.

1994 MUSTANG COUPE
The rear of '94–95 Mustangs featured a horizontal three-element taillight design of which purists did not approve.

1995 MUSTANG GT
The 1995 GT outsold the 1994 GT by more than 10,000 units. This could be because '95 saw the first full 12 months of production. The fact that the GT was quite an affordable package at a base price of just over $18,000 did not hurt either.

MIRRORS
Dual electric remote-control mirrors were standard on all Mustangs for 1994–95

NO 5.0
The "5.0" emblem found on the last generation was replaced by a "GT Mustang" emblem

HOOD SCOOPS
1994–95 Mustangs had these functional hood scoops, similar to those on the Mach III concept car

SCOOP
The scoop and scallop returned to the side for the 1994 model year

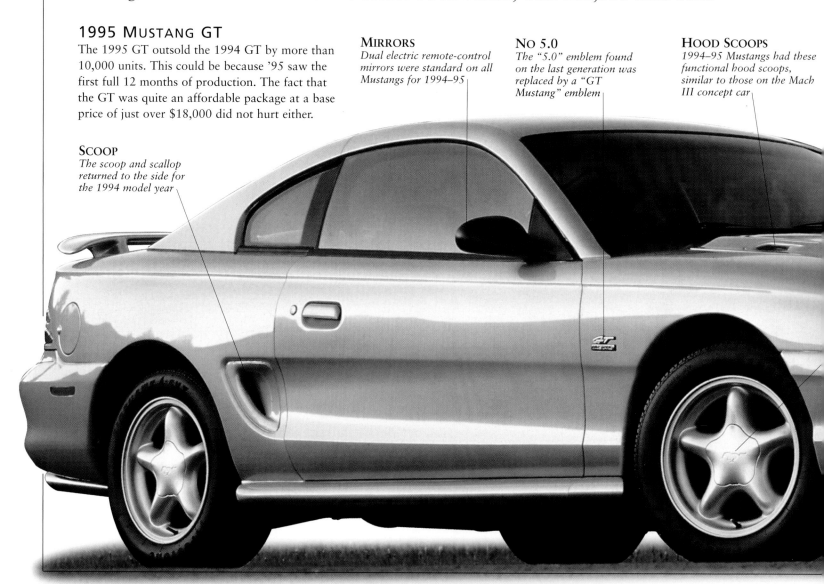

1994 Mustang SVT Cobra

The SVT Cobra model would return in greater numbers for 1994. It would become the top performance Mustang for the next several years.

Paint
1994 SVT Cobras were available only in red, white, or black

Rear Spoiler
Cobra models had a different rear spoiler that included a built-in LED stop lamp

Wheels
SVT Cobras featured unique 17"x 10" polished-aluminum wheels

Brakes
Cobras featured larger brakes with 13-inch discs in front and 11.65-inch discs on the rear

KEY FEATURES
1995 Mustang GT Coupe

- **Production:** 47,088 units
- **Standard front fog lamps**
- **Rear spoiler**
- **16-inch cast-aluminum wheels**
- **5.0L V-8 standard engine**

1995 Mustang Interior
The interior remained unchanged for the 1995 model year; driver and passenger air bags were standard.

THE LAST 5.0 LITER

1995 marked the last year that the tried-and-true 5.0L engine would be installed in new Mustangs. The Windsor small-block engine had been a part of the Mustang line since 1964. Ford gave the engine a farewell by upping horsepower to 240 and installing the SVT "GT-40" cylinder head and intake manifold combination. Larger valves and a more radical camshaft were also used. The 240 hp 5.0L was limited to the SVT Cobra, but the 215 hp version lived its last days in the Mustang GT.

Wheels
These 16-inch five-spoke wheels were standard on GTs

Fog Lamps
The Mustang GT package continued to include driving lamps

The 240 hp 5.0L used special "GT-40" components

1996 SVT Cobra

1996 COBRA EMBLEM

THE BIG NEWS FOR 1996 MODELS was the availability of the 4.6L, single overhead cam, modular V-8 engine that produced 215 hp. SVT Cobra models featured a dual overhead cam version of the 4.6L engine that pumped out 305 hp. Thus, for the first time in many years, the Mustang's horsepower rating matched that of its fiercest rival, the Chevrolet Camaro. All engines had platinum-tipped spark plugs with a 100,000-mile life span, eliminating the need for tune-ups. Taillights reverted to a vertical three-element design. SVT Cobras came in four colors: Laser Red, Crystal White, Black, and Mystic. Depending on the lighting and the viewing angle, Mystic paint could look blue, purple, or green. For an upper-end Mustang, the SVT Cobra sold well. Sales for 1996 were 10,006 units.

INSTRUMENT PANEL
White gauge faces reminiscent of the 1950s graced the instrument panel of SVT Mustangs.

SVT SPEED

With more than 300 hp, the SVT Cobra could turn a quarter-mile time of less than 14 seconds, making it one of the fastest Mustangs in nearly 30 years. Convertibles accounted for only about one quarter of SVT Cobra sales, making them very desirable today.

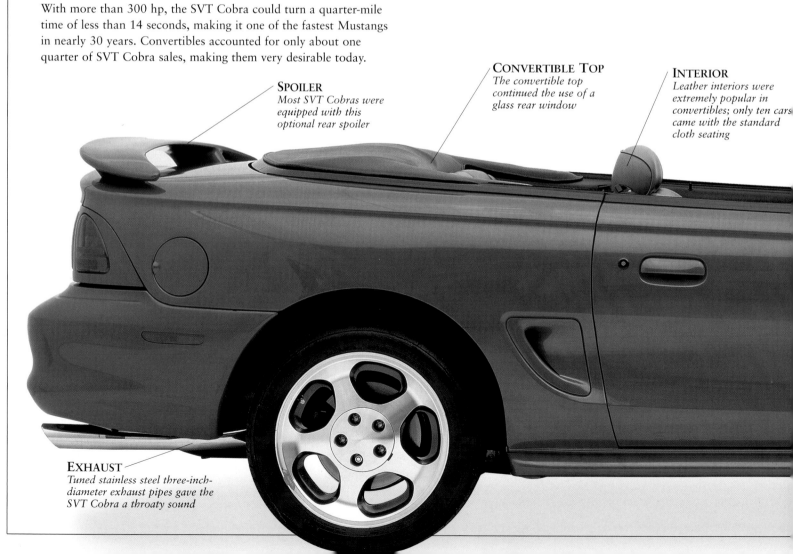

SPOILER
Most SVT Cobras were equipped with this optional rear spoiler

CONVERTIBLE TOP
The convertible top continued the use of a glass rear window

INTERIOR
Leather interiors were extremely popular in convertibles; only ten cars came with the standard cloth seating

EXHAUST
Tuned stainless steel three-inch-diameter exhaust pipes gave the SVT Cobra a throaty sound

THE NEW 4.6L DOHC ENGINE

Mustang SVT Cobra received an all-new engine for 1996. The 4.6L DOHC used four valves per cylinder and dual overhead camshafts per bank of cylinders. Producing 305 hp, these were and still are the most powerful engines installed in a Mustang in the last 25 years. The engines are hand-assembled in a special area of the Romeo, Michigan, engine plant by 12 two-man teams. When assembly is complete, the men sign their names to a plaque and attach it to the left cam cover.

The 4.6L DOHC engine

KEY FEATURES
1996 Mustang SVT Cobra

- **Production:** 2,510 units (convertible)
- **First year for 4.6L DOHC engine**
- **New Borg-Warner T45 five-speed transmission**
- **Revised taillights**
- **New domed hood**

The 4.6L DOHC engine was a tight fit in the Mustang Cobra

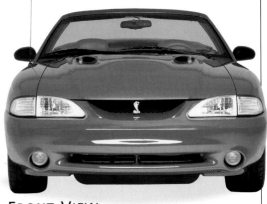

FRONT VIEW

All SVT Cobra models had a more aggressive front end with round fog lamps mounted low and snake emblem mounted in the grille.

REAR STYLING

The taillight panel featured vertical taillights, replacing the horizontal units of '94–95. "Cobra" was debossed into the bumper.

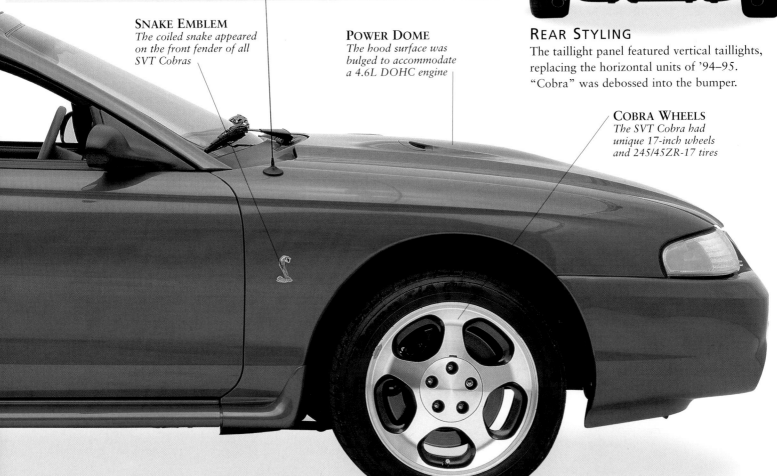

SNAKE EMBLEM
The coiled snake appeared on the front fender of all SVT Cobras

POWER DOME
The hood surface was bulged to accommodate a 4.6L DOHC engine

COBRA WHEELS
The SVT Cobra had unique 17-inch wheels and 245/45ZR-17 tires

1996–1998 Mustang Variations

FEW SIGNIFICANT CHANGES WERE INTRODUCED to Mustang after 1996. Coupe and convertible body styles in base and GT configurations continued to be offered in ten colors each year; SVT Cobra models had a more limited palette of four or five choices. Interiors could be enhanced by leather covering on sport bucket seats. An electronic AM/FM stereo unit became standard on all models, and a premium sound system with cassette player and more power was available. Auto audiophiles could opt for a Mach 460 system and specify a compact disc player to take advantage of the 460-watt amplifier. Base models came with the V-6 engine; GTs got the modular V-8.

1996 GT CONVERTIBLE
Those wanting a low profile did not choose Bright Tangerine, a 1996-only color.

BODY STYLE
The GT body u
exactly the same
1997 as in 1996

1997 MUSTANG GT
The GT did not change much for 1997. A revised security system became standard on all models, and the standard interior received new flecked fabric. Leather seating continued to be an option.

JJT 236

MUSTANG GT

BUMPER DETAIL
"Mustang" was debossed
into the rear bumper

- **Production:** 18,464 units

- **Body style virtually unchanged for 1997**

- **New security system**

- **New upholstery fabric**

- **Leather seating optional**

NEW COLOR
Buyers could order Canary Yellow on 1998 Mustang Cobras

1998 SVT COBRA
Of all the models in the Mustang line for 1998, the SVT Cobra changed the most. New 17-inch, five-spoke wheels replaced the five-hole wheels in place since 1994. Two new colors were introduced for the Cobra: Canary Yellow and Bright Atlantic Blue.

FRONT FASCIA
The front fascia on Cobra models continued to be more aggressive than on standard or even GT models

NEW WHEELS
1998 Cobras used new five-spoke 17-inch wheels

THE 4.6L SOHC ENGINE

Ford's modular engine program began in the late 1980s. The concept was to create an engine design that could produce V-6 and V-8 engines with the same tooling. The two-valve 4.6L SOHC V-8 engine first appeared in 1991 Ford full-size cars. The 4.6L SOHC replaced the Windsor-built 5.0L in Mustangs for the 1996 model year. The 4.6L was shorter and somewhat lighter than the 34-year-old engine from Canada. The chain-driven overhead camshafts (one for each bank of cylinders) were mounted to aluminum cylinder heads and activated two valves for each cylinder. Cam covers were molded plastic, and the cylinder block was cast iron. The 4.6L was rated at 215 hp for its introduction, the same rating as the previous 5.0L, but would grow in power as it matured.

SMOOTHER ENGINE
The 4.6L engine ran more smoothly than the 5.0L used in Mustang models before 1996

BIG WHEELS
The GT could be ordered with these 17-inch wheels that debuted for the '96 model year

NEW EMBLEM
A new GT emblem read "4.6," replacing the "Mustang" found on earlier models

The 4.6L SOHC replaced the 5.0L as the standard V-8 in 1996

1999 Mustang

35TH ANNIVERSARY EMBLEM

FORD'S PONY CAR CELEBRATED its 35th anniversary in 1999. As of that date, no other nameplate in Ford's stable had a longer continuous production run except Thunderbird. Ford had created a legend in automotive history and proclaimed the car's ancestry in its advertising and sales brochures. Mustang dressed for the party in a freshened body design that gave an edgy, more contemporary look to the now five-year-old body shell. A new centrally positioned, nonfunctional single scoop appeared on the hood with a honeycomb pattern insert that matched the taller and equally nonfunctional side scallop scoop inset.

MUSTANG CONVERTIBLE
The 1999 convertible was compared to the original 1964½ in Ford promotional materials. New angular taillights continued the three-element design.

35TH ANNIVERSARY MUSTANG GT
Ford celebrated the 35th anniversary of the Mustang with this limited-edition model. Only available as a GT, it featured additional blacked-out trim and a special silver-and-black leather interior.

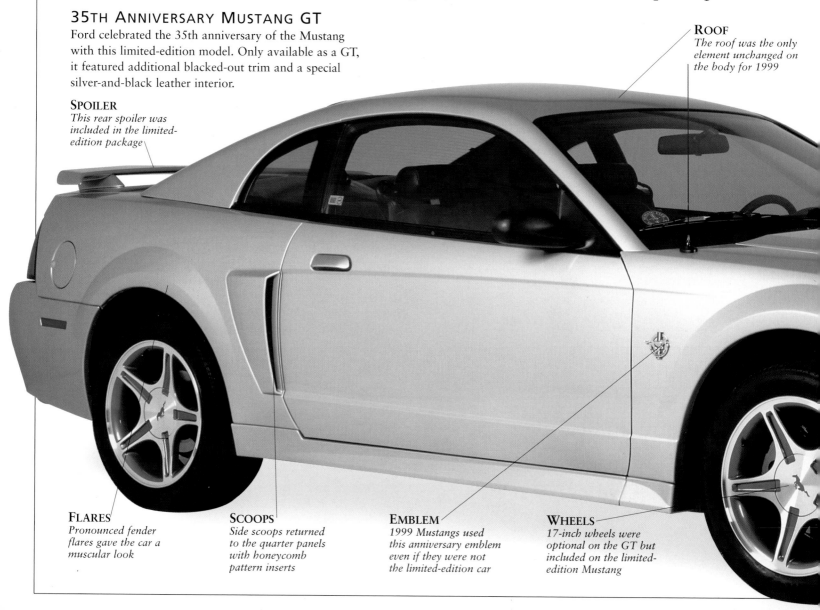

SPOILER
This rear spoiler was included in the limited-edition package

ROOF
The roof was the only element unchanged on the body for 1999

FLARES
Pronounced fender flares gave the car a muscular look

SCOOPS
Side scoops returned to the quarter panels with honeycomb pattern inserts

EMBLEM
1999 Mustangs used this anniversary emblem even if they were not the limited-edition car

WHEELS
17-inch wheels were optional on the GT but included on the limited-edition Mustang

SVT COBRA INDEPENDENT REAR SUSPENSION

SVT Cobra models for 1999 incorporated a revolutionary (for Mustang) new independent rear suspension (IRS), with asplit rear axle. Every Mustang preceding it had a solid rear axle. A revised floorpan allowed the new suspension, adapted from the Lincoln Mark VIII, to mount in the same location as the solid axle that was still being used on the GT and base models. Although the new suspension was heavier, its contemporary design provided more precise handling and improved ride quality.

The new SVT Cobra suspension improved handling by allowing the car's rear tires to move independently of each other

Springs were much stiffer than the solid axle to allow for better handling

Upper contol arms are made of steel to add strength

The axle is split into two seperate parts at the differential, enabling the tires to move independently of each other.

Lower control arms are made of aluminum for lighter weight

These brackets mount the IRS into the solid axle's lower control arm brackets

This artist's rendering of the 1999 suspension system shows the design and arrangement of the new system's parts

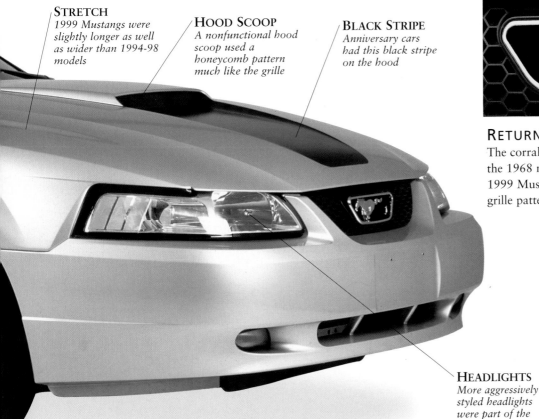

STRETCH
1999 Mustangs were slightly longer as well as wider than 1994-98 models

HOOD SCOOP
A nonfunctional hood scoop used a honeycomb pattern much like the grille

BLACK STRIPE
Anniversary cars had this black stripe on the hood

HEADLIGHTS
More aggressively styled headlights were part of the '99 makeover

RETURN OF THE CORRAL
The corralled pony emblem had not been seen since the 1968 models. Ford returned this icon to the 1999 Mustang and incorporated a honeycomb grille pattern reminiscent of the 1965 model.

KEY FEATURES

1999 Mustang Anniversary GT

- **Production:** 9,256 units
- **Updated body design**
- **Special black-and-silver interior**
- **All new traction control available**
- **More powerful engines available**

2000–2001 Mustang Variations

WITH A MAJOR BODY RESTYLE FOR 1999, the base model Mustang and Mustang GT did not change very much for the year 2000. A slight fender badge change and a couple of new colors were additions. Buyers wanting something different went for one of performance specialist Steve Saleen's 360 hp S281-SC Mustangs. These Mustangs on steroids have been noted for their modified engines, Racecraft suspension components, gigantic alloy wheels, and many appearance refinements. Hardly a part of the car did not receive the Saleen touch, yet a full Ford warranty was provided to the owner. Those wanting more nostalgia might have opted for a 2001 Bullitt GT. This special edition was a hopped-up Mustang repackaging of the 1968 GT that "starred" in the movie *Bullitt*.

2000 MUSTANG
The Mustang for 2000 did not change very much. The most obvious change was the removal of the anniversary emblem from the front fender.

2000 SALEEN S281-SC
Steve Saleen continued to produce high-performance Mustangs. The S281-SC was his top-of-the-line 2000 Mustang, able to jump from 0 to 60 mph in under five seconds, out-performing cars costing more than twice the $38,000 base price.

HOOD
A special lightweight hood could be ordered to improve engine cooling

HEADLIGHTS
The S281-SC used the same headlights found on regular Mustangs

VENTS
These vents added downforce by allowing air to escape from under the car

FRONT VALANCE
The S281-SC had a lower front valance with large air intakes

BULLITT, THE CAR

In 1968, Steve McQueen played police detective Frank Bullitt in the movie of the same name, *Bullitt*. To Mustang fans, however, the real star of the movie was the green 1968 Mustang GT in which Lt. Bullitt chased the bad guys' Dodge Charger for nine minutes through the streets of San Francisco in one of the most gripping chase scenes ever filmed. To capitalize on the continued cult status of the car, Ford introduced a special-edition "Bullitt" Mustang for mid-year 2001. The Bullitt GT featured lowered suspension, special gas cap, metal pedal pads, and brushed-aluminum shift knob. Engine modifications added up to 15 more hp to help catch the bad guys.

A special "Bullitt" emblem graced the rear panel between the taillights

The interior featured metal racing-type pedals and a machined aluminum shifter

6,500 Bullitt GTs were available in black, blue, or, as Frank Bullitt would have it, dark green

The Bullitt GT featured new five-spoke wheels with dark spokes similar to those found on the original car

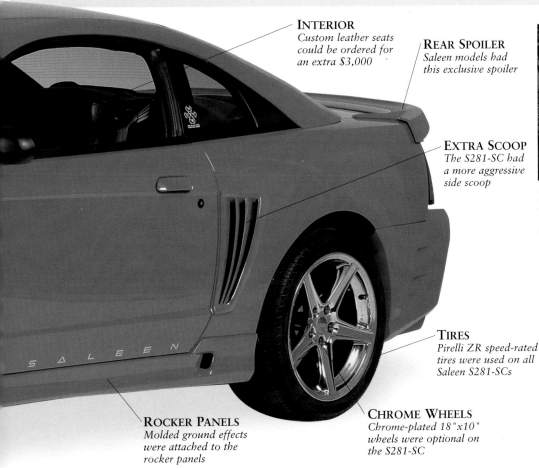

INTERIOR
Custom leather seats could be ordered for an extra $3,000

REAR SPOILER
Saleen models had this exclusive spoiler

EXTRA SCOOP
The S281-SC had a more aggressive side scoop

TIRES
Pirelli ZR speed-rated tires were used on all Saleen S281-SCs

ROCKER PANELS
Molded ground effects were attached to the rocker panels

CHROME WHEELS
Chrome-plated 18"x10" wheels were optional on the S281-SC

SC IS FOR SUPERCHARGED

The S281-SC's 4.6L DOHC engine was equipped with a supercharger.

KEY FEATURES

2000 Saleen S281-SC

- **Production:** 435 units
- **Designed by Steve Saleen**, race driver and performance engineer
- 4.6L DOHC supercharged engine
- Distinctive Saleen body panels
- 18" wheels and Pirelli Tires

1994–2001 Trans-Am Racing

AT THE TURN OF THE MILLENNIUM, Mustang continued the road-racing renaissance that began in the previous decade and pushed toward even higher goals. With the involvement of racing magicians Jack Roush and Steve Saleen, Mustang dominated the Trans-Am series in the '90s and became a true world contender in road racing, with a record of success that continues today. In 1994 the Jack Roush Racing and Tom Gloy Racing teams collected enough wins to earn Ford the Manufacturers' Cup. Driver Tom Kendall owned the Trans-Am series in the 1990s, piloting Roush Racing Mustangs. The Saleen/Allen Speed Lab RRR team has excelled in SCCA's World Challenge class. The team, including television and movie star Tim Allen, won the SCCA World Challenge Manufacturers' Championship in 1996 and continues to be successful to date.

BURNING UP THE TRACK
Mustang continued to rack up titles in 1999 by winning all the races. Paul Gentilozzi won the drivers championship in this HomeLink-sponsored Mustang.

THE YEAR OF KENDALL
In 1997, Tom Kendall became one of the most dominant drivers in Trans-Am history piloting the Roush Racing No.11 All Sport-sponsored Mustangs. He won a record-setting 11 races in that year.

2000 SALEEN/ALLEN RACE TEAM

The Saleen Mustang sponsored by driver/actor Tim Allen's "Home Improvement" TV show took the manufacturers' and team championships in the Grand American division in 2000.

ROUSH MAKES MUSTANG HISTORY

In the 1994 Trans-Am season opener in Miami, the Roush Racing team became the first in Trans-Am history to reach 50 wins. Tom Kendall piloted the winning Mustang in a flag-to-flag victory.

1997 TOM GLOY RACING

In 1997, nobody could touch Tom Kendall, not even 1989 champ Dorsey Schroeder. Schroeder would pilot Tom Gloy-prepared Mustangs to seven top fives and a fifth-place finish in the final point standings.

THE AMAZING TOM KENDALL

Still in his thirties, Tommy Kendall has a Mustang racing record that looks like the combined lifetime achievements of three drivers. Through the decade of the 1990s and into the next century, he has continued to break records and dominate the Trans-Am series as if no one ever told him he was allowed not to win a race. In 1994 at the Trans-Am season opener in Miami, he nailed a flag-to-flag win that made the Roush Racing team the first in history to accrue 50 wins. In 1997 he set new records for total wins, most consecutive wins (breaking Mark Donohue's record of 8 by taking 11 in a row), and most Trans-Am championships. He won the Trans-Am title in 1995, 1996, and 1997 driving a Roush-built Mustang Cobra. In 1995 he made a splash by winning the IMSA 24 Hours of Daytona teamed with partners Mark Martin and actor Paul Newman. Kendall continues to race on a limited schedule in select NASCAR Winston Cup and Craftsman Truck series road races.

Tom Kendall leads the pack at Mid-Ohio in 1994. He would go on to win that event, one of four wins for him that year

1994–2001 Memorabilia

COLLECTIBLES AND MEMORABILIA with Mustang themes continue to provide owners and fans with items to personalize their cars' appearance and enjoy at home. Games, clothing, personal items, and accessories in a multitude of styles are all available to the devoted Mustanger. For the Mustang's 35th Anniversary, Ford pulled out the stops. Included with the purchase of the special GT anniversary model was an array of free goodies, and owners could buy die-cast replicas of their own cars. Kit manufacturers from the US and abroad have loaded up car modelers with a variety of offerings since the fourth-generation Mustang's debut in 1994. Never in the history of the Mustang has such a high volume and wide variety of merchandise been available to enthusiasts.

MUSTANG MONOPOLY

Parker Brothers in 1999 released a version of Monopoly, the popular real-estate game, tailored to the Mustang fan. Players try to get rich buying, renting, or selling Mustangs. Those familiar with the game will appreciate how the Mustang's history has been incorporated with special "Chance" and "Community Chest" cards, carports and garages replacing the houses and hotels, and Ford dealerships replacing railroads.

GAME PIECES

Mustang Monopoly game tokens include a "Ford Benzoil" gasoline pump, horseshoe, 1999 coupe, 1965 steering wheel, styled steel wheel and tire, 1964½ convertible, 1965 fastback, and 1965 front fascia, all rendered in pewter.

ANNIVERSARY SURPRISE

1999 Mustang purchasers received a box of goodies in the mail soon after taking delivery of their cars. The intention was to "surprise and delight" new owners with three music CDs and a vinyl CD storage pouch.

1994 POSTER

This poster illustrated the similarities between the 1994 and '64½ models.

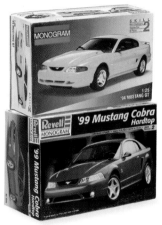

SCALE REPLICAS

From model kits to assembled die-casts, replicas of 1994–2001 are widely available at retail stores.

MUSTANG SPECIALTY ITEMS

All kinds of accessories are available for the real die-hard Mustang collector. These include watches, money clips, and keychains.

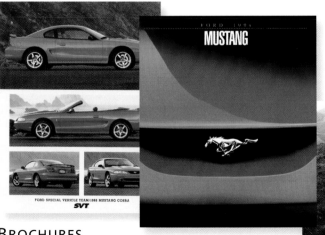

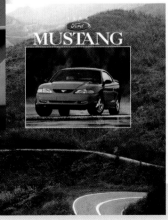

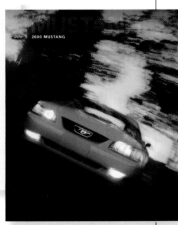

BROCHURES

Brochures continue to be collected by the Mustang enthusiast. Ford also produced a special brochure for the SVT Cobra for these years. Those wanting to get started can visit their local Ford dealership to pick up the most current brochure.

Glossary

AA/FC

A drag racing classification. The first "A" ranks the car highest in power-to-weight ratio; the second "A" means supercharged; "FC" stands for fuel coupe.

ABS

Anti-Lock Brake System.

A/FX

A/Factory Experimental.
(See AA/FC above.)

AHRA

American Hot Rod Association.

Airdam

An aerodynamic skirt that is usually placed under the front bumper.

A-pillars

The first set of structural roof supports at either side of the windshield.

Beltline

The horizontal area of a vehicle's body that runs along the door just below the side-window glass.

Bezel

An ornamental, shaped, often bright edging found around a functional body part such as an emblem, gauge, or light.

B-pillar

On a two-door sedan, the often structural vertical sheetmetal that separates the door glass from the rear quarter-window glass.

Bushing

A tubular part that, when mounted in a housing, acts as a bearing or as insulation from abrasion.

CAFE

Corporate Average Fuel Economy; laws mandating minimum fuel economy standards that took effect in 1978.

Camshaft

One of a number of shafts in an engine that open and close the valves.

Coupe

A closed two-door car.

Chassis

The structural framework of a car, which includes the axles, drivetrain, engine, steering, and suspension.

CHMSL

Center High Mounted Stop Light (pronounced Chimsel).

Clear coat

The clear protective coating applied in a base coat/clear coat or tri-coat system. The clear coat can be an acrylic lacquer or an enamel.

Coefficient of drag (Cd)

A numerical value that represents aerodynamic efficiency. The lower the value, the more efficient the shape.

Cowl

The structural body part located at the front of the passenger compartment, between the engine hood and the body, back to the windshield.

C-pillar

The area of sheetmetal where the rear of the roof connects to the body.

Cubic inch displacement (cid)

The volume of space in an engine's cylinders.

Decklid

The lid of the luggage compartment (trunk).

Die-casting

To produce a part by pouring a molten metal alloy, into a mold.

DOHC

Dual Overhead Camshafts

Drag slicks

Wide, high-performance tires used on race cars.

Drivetrain

Also known as the powertrain, the parts between the engine and the driving wheels, including the clutch, transmission driveshaft, and rear axle.

Fascia

The flexible material that covers a car's bumper.

Fastback

A body shape in which the roof slopes downward at the rear and meets the deck or luggage compartment with no notch or visual break.

F/C

A racing classification that technically stands for Fuel Coupe but in popular lexicon translates to "funny car."

Firewall

A sheetmetal panel that separates the engine compartment from the passenger compartment.

Flared fender

A fender to which material has been added around the wheelwell so that the fenders cover wide tires.

Funny car

A type of drag racing car with a wheel base altered from production length and no doors. Usually has a fiberglass body and supercharged engine. The term evolved out of its official racing designation as AA/FC (fuel coupe).

Ground effects

Styling touches around the lower body edge of a car.

GTP

Grand Touring Prototype.

Hardtop

A body style that lacks the B-pillar so that although the roof is rigid (usually steel), it has the configuration of a convertible.

Hi-Po
Ford's nickname for its 289cid High Performance engine, a powerful V-8 available as of 1965.

HP
Horsepower.

IFS
Independent Front Suspension.

IHRA
International Hot Rod Association.

IMSA
International Motor Sports Association.

IRS
Independent Rear Suspension.

Lip molding
Ornamental bright trim that outlines and visually reinforces a fender wheel opening. Also called wheel molding.

Louvers
A series of slits in the body of a vehicle that allows air in or out. Also used on body panels for decoration.

Marker lights
The lights mounted on the fenders of a car that mark its outside boundaries and corners.

Musclecar
A stock vehicle with greater than usual horsepower.

NHRA
National Hot Rod Association.

Notchback
A body style in which the upright backlight joins a primarily horizontal rear deck, the resulting joint forming a notch.

NASA ducts
Air ducts, usually on the hood of a car, derived from a design originally used by the National Aeronautics and Space Administration.

Pillar
A structural, upright body member that separates the doors or windows.

Platform
The engineering basis for a car. The word may be applied to both the car in theory during its planning stages and to the finished car.

Prototype
A realistic, sometimes functional, full-sized, three-dimensional representation of an entire car made prior to production.

Quarter panel
The part of a car body-side that is comprised of the rear fender from the rear door opening to the back of the car.

Quarter window
A small, usually movable glass pane located next to a larger window that directs the air into, or out of, the interior.

Rocker
The lengthwise sill that runs beneath the doors and along the bottom of the body.

SCCA
Sports Car Club of America.

Scoop
An area of the body that is open-fronted and designed to let in air.

Sedan
A car with two or four doors. Two-door sedans are distinguished from hardtops by the presence of a B-pillar.

SOHC
Single Overhead Camshafts.

Spoiler
A low wing, usually affixed to the top rear surface of the decklid. On race cars, its function is to reduce aerodynamic lift. On production cars the spoiler is often ornamental.

Subframe
The chassis structure that carries the engine and/or suspension, and is bolted or welded to the front or rear underside of a unitized body.

SVO
The Special Vehicle Operations division of Ford; the term also applied to the cars developed by this division.

SVT
The Special Vehicle Team, a division of Ford that, like its predecessor the SVO, was created to develop cars to compete with imported sports coupes.

Targa
A type of car top that allows center and rear roof sections to be removed for open-air riding, leaving a central roof bar for passenger protection.

Top boot
The cover that goes over a lowered convertible top.

Track
The center-to-center distance between both front or both rear tires, or wheels. Also known as Tread.

T-roof
A car featuring removable glass roof panels over the two front seats.

Unitized body
That type of construction in which the frame and body of the car form a single unit. Also referred to as "frame-integral."

Valance
A panel that hangs down below the bumper and is intended to hide the chassis and undersurface of the car.

VIN
Vehicle Identification Number. The identification code number assigned to an individual car by the factory; usually appearing on a plate affixed to the driver's door or dashboard.

Wheelbase
The distance between the front and rear axle centerlines.

Wheelcover
A protective, ornamental disc of metal that covers an entire wheel. Different from a hubcap, which covers only the center of the wheel.

Wire wheel
A type of wheel with a steel rim and multiple, interlaced wire spokes attached to a center hub.

Technical Data

1964½–1965

The Ford Mustangs built between March 1964 and August 17, 1964, were known as early 1965 or 1964½ Mustangs. Those that were built after August 17, 1964, were known as late 1965 Mustangs.

PRODUCTION FIGURES

1964½

Convertible, standard	28,833
Coupe, standard	92,705
Total	**121,538**

1965

Convertible, standard	65,663
Convertible, bench seats	2,111
Convertible, luxury	5,338
Coupe, standard	372,123
Coupe, bench seats	14,905
Coupe, luxury	22,232
Fastback, standard	71,303
Fastback, luxury	5,776
Total	**559,451**

RETAIL PRICES

Convertible, standard	$2,557
Coupe, standard	$2,320
Fastback, standard	$2,533

EXTERIOR COLORS

Cascade Green (1964½)
Caspian Blue (1964½ & 1965)
Champagne Beige (1965)
Chantilly Beige (1964½)
Dynasty Green (1964½)
Guardsman Blue (1964½)
Honey Gold (1965)
Ivy Green (1965)
Midnight Turquoise (1965)
Pagoda Green (1964½)
Phoenician Yellow (1964½)
Poppy Red (1964½ & 1965)
Prairie Bronze (1964½ & 1965)
Rangoon Red (1964½ & 1965)
Raven Black (1964½ & 1965)
Silver Blue (1965)
Silversmoke Gray (1964½ & 1965)
Skylight Blue (1964½)
Springtime Yellow (1965)
Sunlight Yellow (1964½ & 1965)
Tropical Turquoise (1965)
Twilight Turquoise (1964½)
Vintage Burgundy (1964½ & 1965)
Wimbledon White (1964½ & 1965)

ENGINE CODES

170cid 1V 6 cyl 101 hp (1964½)	U
200cid 1V 6 cyl 120 hp (1965)	T
260cid 2V V-8 164 hp (1964½)	F
289cid 2V V-8 200 hp (1965)	C
289cid 4V V-8 210 hp (1964½)	D
289cid 4V V-8 225 hp (1965)	A
289cid 4V V-8 271 hp high performance (1965)	K

VEHICLE IDENTIFICATION NUMBERS

5	Last digit of model year (1965)
T	Assembly plant (F-Dearborn, R-San Jose, T-Metuchen)
07	Body code for coupe (08-convertible, 09-fastback)
F	Engine code
100001	Consecutive unit number

For example: 5T07F100001

1965 SHELBY MUSTANG

Shelby Mustangs of this era carried two VINs, one for Shelby and one for Ford.

PRODUCTION FIGURES

Competition models (R)	36
Racing and special models	12
Street production models	516
Total	**564**

RETAIL PRICES

Race	$5,995
Street	$4,547

EXTERIOR COLOR

Wimbledon White

ENGINE CODE

289cid 4V V-8 271 hp high performance	K

VEHICLE IDENTIFICATION NUMBERS - SHELBY

SFM	Shelby Ford Mustang
5	Last digit of model year
S	(S-Street, R-Race)
001	Consecutive unit number

For example: SFM5S001

VEHICLE IDENTIFICATION NUMBERS - FORD

5	Last digit of model year
R	Assembly plant (R-San Jose)
09	Body code (for fastback)
K	Engine code
000001	Consecutive unit number

For example: 5R09K000001

1966

PRODUCTION FIGURES

Convertible, standard	56,409
Convertible, bench seats	3,190
Convertible, luxury	12,520
Coupe, standard	422,416
Coupe, bench seats	21,397
Coupe, luxury	55,938
Fastback, standard	27,809
Fastback, luxury	7,889
Total	**607,568**

RETAIL PRICES

Convertible, standard	$2,652
Coupe, standard	$2,416
Fastback, standard	$2,607

EXTERIOR COLORS

Antique Bronze
Arcadian Blue
Brittany Blue
Candy Apple Red
Dark Moss Green (late 1966)
Emberglo
Ivy Green Metallic
Nightmist Blue
Raven Black
Sahara Beige
Sauterne Gold
Signalflare Red
Silver Blue
Silver Frost
Springtime Yellow
Tahoe Turquoise
Vintage Burgundy
Wimbledon White

ADDITIONAL AVAILABLE COLORS

Light Beige
Maroon Metallic
Medium Palomino Metallic
Medium Silver Metallic
Silver Blue Metallic

ENGINE CODES

200cid 1V 6 cyl 120 hp	T
289cid 2V V-8 200 hp	C
289cid 4V V-8 225 hp	A
289cid 4V V-8 271 hp	K

VEHICLE IDENTIFICATION NUMBERS

6	Last digit of model year
R	Assembly plant (F-Dearborn, R-San Jose, T-Metuchen)
07	Body code for coupe (08-convertible, 09-fastback)
C	Engine code
100001	Consecutive unit number

For example: 6R07C100001

1966 SHELBY MUSTANG

PRODUCTION FIGURES

GT350	1,368
GT350 Convertibles	4
GT350H Hertz rental cars	1,001
GT350 Race cars	4
Total	**2,377**

RETAIL PRICES

Shelby GT350	$4,428

EXTERIOR COLORS

Candy Apple Red
Ivy Green
Raven Black
Sapphire Blue
Wimbledon White

ENGINE CODE

289cid 4V V-8 271 hp high performance	K

VEHICLE IDENTIFICATION NUMBERS - SHELBY

SFM	Shelby Ford Mustang
6	Last digit of model year
S	(S-Street, R-Race)
0001	Consecutive unit number

For example: SFM6S0001

VEHICLE IDENTIFICATION NUMBERS - FORD

6	Last digit of model year
R	Assembly plant (R-San Jose)
09	Body code (for fastback)
K	Engine code
00001	Consecutive unit number

For example: 6R09K00001

1967

PRODUCTION FIGURES

Convertible, standard	38,751
Convertible, bench seats	1,209
Convertible, luxury	4,848
Coupe, standard	325,853
Coupe, bench seats	8,190
Coupe, luxury	22,228
Fastback, standard	53,651
Fastback, luxury	17,391
Total	**472,121**

RETAIL PRICES

Convertible, standard	$2,898
Coupe, standard	$2,461
Fastback, standard	$2,692

EXTERIOR COLORS

Acapulco Blue	Frost Turquoise
Arcadian Blue	Lime Gold
Brittany Blue	Nightmist Blue
Burnt Amber	Pebble Beige
Candy Apple Red	Raven Black
Clearwater Aqua	Sauterne Gold
Dark Moss Green	Silver Frost
Diamond Blue	Springtime Yellow
Diamond Green	Vintage Burgundy
Dusk Rose	Wimbledon White

ADDITIONAL AVAILABLE COLORS

Anniversary Gold	Columbine Blue
Aspen Gold	Lavender
Blue Bonnet	Playboy Pink
Bright Red	Timberline Green

ENGINE CODES

200cid 1V 6 cyl 120 hp	U
289cid 2V V-8 200 hp	C
289cid 4V V-8 225 hp	A
289cid 4V V-8 271 hp	K
390cid 4V V-8 320 hp	S

VEHICLE IDENTIFICATION NUMBERS

7	Last digit of model year
F	Assembly plant (F-Dearborn, R-San Jose, T-Metuchen)
01	Body code for coupe (02-fastback, 03-convertible)
C	Engine code
100001	Consecutive unit number

For example: 7F01C100001

1967 SHELBY MUSTANG

PRODUCTION FIGURES

GT350	1,175
GT500	2,048
Special models	2
Total	**3,225**

RETAIL PRICES

GT350	$3,995
GT500	$4,195

EXTERIOR COLORS

Brittany Blue	Medium Metallic Gray
Bronze Metallic	Raven Black
Dark Blue Metallic	Red
Dark Moss Green	Silver Frost
Lime Green	Wimbledon White
Medium Blue/Acapulco Blue	

ENGINE CODES

289cid 4V V-8 271 hp	K
428cid 4V V-8 335 hp	Q

VEHICLE IDENTIFICATION NUMBERS - SHELBY

67	Last two digits of model year
4	Engine (2-289, 4-428)
1	Transmission (0-4-speed, 1-automatic)
0	Base vehicle component
	0 - base vehicle
	1 - Ford air conditioning
	2 - Thermactor exhaust emission
	3 - air conditioning and Thermactor exhaust
F	Body code (F-fastback)
2	Exterior color code
A	Interior trim
00001	Consecutive unit number

For example: 67410F2A00001

VEHICLE IDENTIFICATION NUMBERS - FORD

7	Last digit of model year
R	Assembly plant (R-San Jose)
02	Body code (02-fastback)
K	Engine code (K-271 hp 289, Q-428 ci)
00001	Consecutive unit number

For example: 7R02K00001

1968

PRODUCTION FIGURES

Convertible, standard	22,037
Convertible, deluxe	3,339
Coupe, standard	233,472
Coupe, bench seats	6,113
Coupe, deluxe	9,009
Coupe, deluxe, bench seats	853
Fastback, standard	33,585
Fastback, bench seats	1,079
Fastback, deluxe	7,661
Fastback, deluxe, bench seats	256
Total	**317,404**

RETAIL PRICES

Convertible, standard	$2,814
Coupe, standard	$2,578
Fastback, standard	$2,689

EXTERIOR COLORS

Acapulco Blue	Pebble Beige
Brittany Blue	Presidential Blue
Candy Apple Red	Royal Maroon
Gulfstream Aqua	Seafoam Green
Highland Green	Sunlit Gold
Lime Gold	Tahoe Turquoise
Meadowlark Yellow	Wimbledon White

ENGINE CODES

200cid 1V 6 cyl l20 hp	T
289cid 2V V-8 195 hp	C
302cid 2V V-8 210 hp	F
302cid 4V V-8 230 hp	J
390cid 4V V-8 325 hp	S
427cid 4V V-8 390 hp	W
428cid 4V V-8 335 hp (CJ)	R

VEHICLE IDENTIFICATION NUMBERS

8	Last digit of model year
R	Assembly plant (F-Dearborn, R-San Jose, T-Metuchen)
01	Body code for coupe (02-fastback, 03-convertible)
J	Engine code
100001	Consecutive unit number

For example: 8R01J100001

1968 SHELBY MUSTANG

Beginning this year, the Shelby had one Ford VIN rather than separate Shelby and Ford numbers. The new single VIN contained a special embedded Shelby code.

PRODUCTION FIGURES

GT350 Convertible	404
GT500 Convertible	402
GT500KR Convertible	318
GT350 Fastback	1,253
GT500 Fastback	1,140
GT500KR Fastback	933
GT500 Special Model	1
Total	**4,451**

RETAIL PRICES

GT350 Convertible	$4,238
GT500 Convertible	$4,438
GT500KR Convertible	$4,594
GT350 Fastback	$4,116
GT500 Fastback	$4,317
GT500KR Fastback	$4,472

EXTERIOR COLORS

Candy Apple Red	Medium Blue Metallic
Dark Blue Metallic	Meadowlark Yellow
Dark Green Metallic	Orange
Gold Metallic	Raven Black
Lime Green Metallic	Wimbledon White

ENGINE CODES

302cid 4V V-8 250 hp	J
428cid 4V V-8 335 hp (Cobra Jet)	R
428cid 4V V-8 360 hp	S

VEHICLE IDENTIFICATION NUMBERS

8	Last digit of model year
T	Assembly plant (T-Metuchen)
03	Body code for convertible (02-fastback)
R	Engine code
000001	Consecutive unit number
00001	Consecutive Shelby production number

For example: 8T03R000001-00001

1968 Fastback

1969

PRODUCTION FIGURES

Convertible, standard	11,307
Convertible, deluxe	3,439
Coupe, standard	118,613
Coupe, bench seats	4,131
Coupe, deluxe	5,210
Coupe, deluxe, bench seats	504
Coupe, Grandé	22,182
Fastback, standard	56,022
Fastback, deluxe	5,958
Fastback, Mach 1	72,458
Total (includes Specials below)	**299,824**

SPECIALS

Boss 429 (includes two Boss Cougars)	869
Boss 302	1,628

RETAIL PRICES

Convertible, standard	$2,832
Coupe, standard	$2,618
Grandé Coupe	$2,849
Fastback, standard	$2,618
Fastback, Mach 1	$3,122

EXTERIOR COLORS

Acapulco Blue	Meadowlark Yellow
Aztec Aqua	New Lime
Black Jade	Pastel Gray
Calypso Coral	Raven Black
Candy Apple Red	Royal Maroon
Champagne Gold	Silver Jade
Gulfstream Aqua	Wimbledon White
Indian Fire Red	Winter Blue
Lime Gold	

ENGINE CODES

200cid 1V 6 cyl 115 hp		T
250cid 1V 6 cyl 155 hp		L
302cid 2V V-8 220 hp		F
302cid 4V V-8 290 hp (Boss)		G
351cid 2V V-8 250 hp		H
351cid 4V V-8 290 hp		M
390cid 4V V-8 320 hp		S
428cid 4V V-8 335 hp (CJ)		Q
428cid 4V V-8 335 hp (CJ-R)		R
429cid 4V V-8 376 hp (Boss)		Z

VEHICLE IDENTIFICATION NUMBERS

9	Last digit of model year
F	Assembly plant (F-Dearborn, R-San Jose, T-Metuchen)
02	Body code for fastback (01-coupe, 03-convertible)
Z	Engine code
100001	Consecutive unit number

For example: 9F02Z100001

1969–70 SHELBY MUSTANG

1969 was the last year for Shelby Mustangs. The unsold 1969 models were rebadged and sold as "updated" 1970 Shelby Mustangs.

PRODUCTION FIGURES

GT350 Convertible	194
GT500 Convertible	335
GT350 Fastback	935
GT500 Fastback	1,536
GT500 Fastback Hertz car	150
Special Models	3
Total 1969–1970 models	**3,153**
(includes 789 updated 1970 models)	

RETAIL PRICES

GT350 Convertible	$4,753
GT500 Convertible	$5,027
GT350 Fastback	$4,434
GT500 Fastback	$4,709

EXTERIOR COLORS

Acapulco Blue	Grabber Yellow
Black Jade	Gulfstream Aqua
Candy Apple Red	Pastel Gray
Grabber Blue	Royal Maroon
Grabber Green	Silver Jade
Grabber Orange	

ENGINE CODES

351cid 4V V-8 290 hp		M
428cid 4V V-8 335 hp (CJ-R)		R

VEHICLE IDENTIFICATION NUMBERS

9	Last digit of model year (0-1970 updated cars)
F	Assembly plant (F-Dearborn)
02	Body code for fastback
M	Engine code (M-351, R-428 CJ-R)
48	Shelby code
0001	Consecutive unit number

For example: 9F02M480001

1970

PRODUCTION FIGURES

Convertible	7,673
Coupe	82,569
Coupe, Grandé	13,581
Fastback	45,934
Fastback Mach 1	40,970
Special, Boss 302	7,013
Special, Boss 429	499
Total	**198,239**

RETAIL PRICES

Convertible, standard	$3,025
Coupe, standard	$2,721
Coupe, Grandé, standard	$2,926
Fastback, standard	$2,771
Fastback, Mach 1, standard	$3,271
Special, Boss 302	$3,720
Special, Boss 429	$4,928

EXTERIOR COLORS

Bright Gold Metallic	Medium Gold Metallic
Calypso Coral	Medium Lime Metallic
Dark Ivy Green Metallic	Pastel Blue
Grabber Blue	Raven Black
Grabber Green	Red
Grabber Orange	Silver Blue Metallic
Light Ivy Yellow	Yellow
Medium Blue Metallic	Wimbledon White

ENGINE CODES

200cid 1V 6 cyl 120 hp		T
250cid 1V 6 cyl 155 hp		L
302cid 2V V-8 220 hp		F
302cid 4V V-8 290 hp (Boss)		G
351cid 2V V-8 250 hp (351W & 351C)		H
351cid 4V V-8 300 hp		M
428cid 4V V-8 335 hp (CJ)		Q
428cid 4V V-8 335 hp (CJ-R)		R
429cid 4V V-8 375 hp (Boss)		Z

VEHICLE IDENTIFICATION NUMBERS

0	Last digit of model year
F	Assembly plant (F-Dearborn, R-San Jose, M-Metuchen)
04	Body code for Grandé (01-coupe, 02-fastback, 03-convertible, 05-Mach 1)
F	Engine code
100001	Consecutive unit number

For example: 0F04F100001

1971

PRODUCTION FIGURES

Convertible	6,121
Coupe	65,696
Coupe, Grandé	17,406
Fastback	23,956
Fastback, Mach 1	36,499
Special, Boss 351	1,806
Total	**151,484**

RETAIL PRICES

Convertible, standard	$3,227
Coupe, standard	$2,911
Coupe, Grandé, standard	$3,117
Fastback, standard	$2,973
Fastback, Mach 1, standard	$3,268
Special, Boss 351	$4,124

EXTERIOR COLORS

Bright Red	Maroon Metallic
Dark Ivy Green Metallic	Medium Brown Metallic
Grabber Blue	Medium Green Metallic
Grabber Green Metallic	Medium Yellow Gold
Grabber Lime	Pastel Blue
Grabber Yellow	Raven Black
Light Gold	Silver Blue Metallic
Light Pewter Metal	Wimbledon White

ADDITIONAL AVAILABLE COLORS

Gold Metallic	Gold Glamour

ENGINE CODES

250cid 1V 6 cyl 145 hp		L
302cid 2V V-8 210 hp		F
351cid 2V V-8 240 hp		H
351cid 4V V-8 280 hp (CJ)		M
351cid 4V V-8 285 hp		M
351cid 4V V-8 330 hp (Boss)		R
429cid 4V V-8 370 hp (CJ)		C
429cid 4V V-8 375 hp (CJ-R)		J

VEHICLE IDENTIFICATION NUMBERS

1	Last digit of model year
T	Assembly plant (F-Dearborn, T-Metuchen)
01	Body code for coupe (02-fastback, 03-convertible, 04-Grand, 05-Mach 1)
M	Engine code
100001	Consecutive unit number

For example: 1T01M100001

1971 Mach I Fastback

1972

PRODUCTION FIGURES

Convertible	6,121
Coupe	57,350
Coupe, Grandé	18,045
Fastback	16,622
Fastback, Mach 1	27,675
Total	**125,813**

RETAIL PRICES

Convertible, standard	$2,965
Coupe, standard	$2,679
Coupe, Grandé, standard	$2,865
Fastback, standard	$2,736
Fastback, Mach 1, standard	$3,003

EXTERIOR COLORS

Bright Blue Metallic	Light Pewter Metallic
Bright Lime	Maroon
Bright Red	Medium Bright Yellow
Dark Green Metallic	Medium Brown Metallic
Gold Glow	Medium Green Metallic
Grabber Blue	Medium Lime Metallic
Ivy Glow	Medium Yellow Gold
Light Blue	Wimbledon White

ENGINE CODES

250cid 1V 6 cyl 98 hp		L
302cid 2V V-8 140 hp		F
351cid 2V V-8 177 hp		H
351cid 4V V-8 266 hp (CJ)		Q
351cid 4V V-8 275 hp (HO)		R

VEHICLE IDENTIFICATION NUMBERS

2	Last digit of model year
F	Assembly plant (F-Dearborn)
05	Body code for Mach I (01-coupe, 02-fastback, 03-convertible, 04-Grandé)
Q	Engine code
100001	Consecutive unit number

For example: 2F05Q100001

1973

PRODUCTION FIGURES

Convertible	11,853
Coupe	51,480
Coupe, Grandé	25,274
Fastback	10,820
Fastback, Mach I	35,440
Total	**134,867**

RETAIL PRICES

Convertible, standard	$3,102
Coupe, standard	$2,760
Coupe, Grandé, standard	$2,946
Fastback, standard	$2,820
Fastback, Mach 1, standard	$3,088

EXTERIOR COLORS

Blue Glow	Medium Blue Metallic
Ivy Glow	Medium Bright Yellow
Bright Red	Medium Brown Metallic
Dark Green Metallic	Medium Copper Metallic
Gold Glow	Medium Green Metallic
Ivy Glow	Medium Yellow Gold
Light Blue	Saddle Bronze Metallic
Medium Aqua	Wimbledon White

ENGINE CODES

250cid 1V 6 cyl 99 hp	L
302cid 2V V-8 141 hp	F
351cid 2V V-8 177 hp	H
351cid 4V V-8 266 hp (CJ)	Q

VEHICLE IDENTIFICATION NUMBERS

3	Last digit of model year
F	Assembly plant (F-Dearborn)
05	Body code for Mach I (01-coupe, 02-fastback, 03-convertible, 04-Grandé)
H	Engine Code
100001	Consecutive unit number

For example: 3F05H100001

1974

PRODUCTION FIGURES

Coupe	177,671
Coupe, Ghia	89,477
Hatchback	74,799
Hatchback, Mach I	44,046
Total	**385,993**

RETAIL PRICES

Coupe, standard	$3,134
Coupe, Ghia, standard	$3,480
Hatchback, standard	$3,328
Hatchback, Mach 1, standard	$3,674

EXTERIOR COLORS

Bright Green Gold Metallic	Medium Copper Metallic
Bright Red	Medium Lime Yellow
Dark Red	Medium Yellow Gold
Ginger Glow	Pearl White
Green Glow	Saddle Bronze Metallic
Light Blue	Silver Metallic
Medium Bright Blue Metallic	Tan Glow

ENGINE CODES

140cid 2.3L 2V 4 cyl 88 hp	Y
171cid 2.8L 2V V-6 105 hp	Z

VEHICLE IDENTIFICATION NUMBERS

4	Last digit of model year
R	Assembly plant (F-Dearborn, R-San Jose)
04	Body code for Ghia (02-coupe, 03-hatchback, 05-Mach 1)
Y	Engine code
100001	Consecutive unit number

For example: 4R04Y100001

1975

PRODUCTION FIGURES

Coupe	85,155
Coupe, Ghia	52,320
Hatchback	30,038
Hatchback, Mach 1	21,062
Total	**188,575**

RETAIL PRICES

Coupe, standard	$3,529
Coupe, Ghia, standard	$3,938
Hatchback, standard	$3,818
Hatchback, Mach 1, standard	$4,188

EXTERIOR COLORS

Black	Light Green
Bright Blue Metallic	Medium Copper Metallic
Bright Red	Pastel Blue
Bright Yellow	Polar White
Dark Brown Metallic	Silver Blue Glow
Dark Red	Silver Metallic
Dark Yellow Green Metallic	Tan Glow
Green Glow	

ENGINE CODES

140cid 2.3L 2V 4 cyl 88 hp	Y
171cid 2.8L 2V V-6 105 hp	Z
302cid 5.0L 2V V-8 140 hp	F

VEHICLE IDENTIFICATION NUMBERS

5	Last digit of model year
F	Assembly plant (F-Dearborn, R-San Jose, T-Metuchen)
02	Body code for coupe (03-hatchback, 04-Ghia, 05-Mach I)
Y	Engine code
100001	Consecutive unit number

For example: 5F02Y100001

1976

PRODUCTION FIGURES

Coupe	78,508
Coupe, Ghia	37,515
Hatchback	62,312
Hatchback, Mach l	9,232
Total	**187,567**

RETAIL PRICES

Coupe, standard	$3,525
Coupe, Ghia, standard	$3,859
Hatchback, standard	$3,781
Hatchback, Mach 1, standard	$4,209

EXTERIOR COLORS

Black	Light Green
Bright Blue Metallic	Medium Chestnut Metallic
Bright Red	Medium Ivy Bronze Metallic
Bright Yellow	Polar White
Dark Brown Metallic	Silver Blue Glow
Dark Red	Silver Metallic
Dark Yellow Green Metallic	Tan Glow

TU-TONE EXTERIOR COLOR COMBINATIONS
BODY COLOR/ACCENT COLOR

Cream/Medium Gold Metallic	White/Bright Red
White/Bright Blue Metallic	

ENGINE CODES

140cid 2.3L 2V 4 cyl 88 hp	Y
171cid 2.8L 2V V-6 105 hp	Z
302cid 5.0L 2V V-8 140 hp	F

VEHICLE IDENTIFICATION NUMBERS

6	Last digit of model year
F	Assembly plant (F-Dearborn, R-San Jose)
04	Body code for Ghia (02-coupe, 03-hatchback, 05-Mach 1)
Y	Engine code
100001	Consecutive unit number

For example: 6F04Y100001

1977

PRODUCTION FIGURES

Coupe	67,783
Coupe, Ghia	29,510
Hatchback	49,161
Hatchback, Mach 1	6,719
Total	**153,173**

RETAIL PRICES

Coupe, standard	$3,678
Coupe, Ghia, standard	$4,096
Hatchback, standard	$3,877
Hatchback, Mach 1, standard	$4,332

EXTERIOR COLORS

Black	Golden Glow
Bright Aqua Glow	Light Aqua Metallic
Bright Red	Medium Emerald Glow
Bright Saddle Metallic	Orange
Bright Yellow	Polar White
Cream	Tan
Dark Brown Metallic	

TU-TONE EXTERIOR COLOR COMBINATIONS
(prior to June 27, 1977)
BODY COLOR/ACCENT COLOR

Cream/Medium Gold Metallic	White/Light Aqua Metallic
White/Bright Red	

ENGINE CODES

140cid 2.3L 2V 4 cyl 92 hp	Y
171cid 2.8L 2V V-6 103 hp	Z
302cid 5.0L 2V V-8 134 hp	F

VEHICLE IDENTIFICATION NUMBERS

7	Last digit of model year
F	Assembly plant (F-Dearborn, R-San Jose)
03	Body code for hatchback (02-coupe, 04-Ghia, 05-Mach 1)
Y	Engine code
100001	Consecutive unit number

For example: 7F03Y100001

1977 Coupe

1978

PRODUCTION FIGURES

Coupe	81,304
Coupe, Ghia	34,730
Hatchback	68,408
Hatchback, Mach 1	7,968
Total	**192,410**

RETAIL PRICES

Coupe, standard	$3,824
Coupe, Ghia, standard	$4,242
Hatchback, standard	$4,088
Hatchback, Mach 1, standard	$4,523

EXTERIOR COLORS

Aqua Glow	Dark Jade Metallic
Aqua Metallic	Dark Midnight Blue
Black	Light Chamois
Bright Red	Medium Chestnut Metallic
Bright Yellow	Polar White
Chamois Glow	Silver Metallic
Dark Brown Metallic	Tangerine

TU-TONE EXTERIOR COLOR COMBINATIONS

BODY COLOR/ACCENT COLOR

Bright Aqua/Metallic White	Silver Metallic/Black
Bright Red/Black	Silver Metallic/Bright Red
Bright Red/White	Tangerine/White
Bright Yellow/Black	White/Aqua Metallic
Dark Jade Metallic/White	White/Black
Light Aqua Metallic/White	White/Bright Red
Light Chamois/Medium Chestnut Metallic	

ENGINE CODES

140cid 2.3L 2V 4 cy1 88 hp	Y
171cid 2.8L 2V V-6 90 hp	Z
302cid 5.0L 2V V-8 139 hp	F

VEHICLE IDENTIFICATION NUMBERS

8	Last digit of model year
R	Assembly plant (F-Dearborn, R-San Jose)
02	Body code for coupe (03-hatchback, 04-Ghia, 05-Mach 1)
Y	Engine code
100001	Consecutive unit number

For example: 8R02Y100001

1979

PRODUCTION FIGURES

Coupe	156,666
Coupe, Ghia	56,351
Hatchback	120,535
Hatchback, Ghia	36,384
Total	**369,936**

RETAIL PRICES

Coupe, standard	$4,494
Coupe, Ghia, standard	$5,064
Hatchback, standard	$4,828
Hatchback, Ghia, standard	$5,216

EXTERIOR COLORS

Black	Medium Chestnut Metallic
Bright Blue	Medium Gray Metallic
Bright Red	Medium Vaquero Gold
Bright Yellow	Polar White
Dark Jade Metallic	Red Glow
Light Chamois	Silver Metallic
Light Medium Blue	Tangerine
Medium Blue Glow	

TU-TONE EXTERIOR COLOR COMBINATIONS

BODY COLOR/ACCENT COLOR

All Black	Silver Metallic/Medium Gray Metallic
Light Medium Blue/Bright Blue	

ENGINE CODES

2.3L 2V 4 cyl 88 hp	Y
2.3L 2V 4 cyl 132 hp (Turbocharged)	W
2.8L 2V V-6 109 hp	Z
3.3L 1V 6 cyl 85 hp	T
5.0L 2V V-8 140 hp	F

VEHICLE IDENTIFICATION NUMBERS

9	Last digit of model year
F	Assembly plant (F-Dearborn, R-San Jose)
02	Body code for coupe (03-hatchback, 04-Ghia, 05-hatchback Ghia)
Y	Engine code
100001	Consecutive unit number

For example: 9F02Y100001

1980

PRODUCTION FIGURES

Coupe	128,893
Coupe, Ghia	23,647
Hatchback	98,497
Hatchback, Ghia	20,285
Total	**271,322**

RETAIL PRICES

Coupe, standard	$5,338
Coupe, Ghia, standard	$5,823
Hatchback, standard	$5,816
Hatchback, Ghia, standard	$5,935

EXTERIOR COLORS

Bittersweet Glow	Dark Chamois Metallic
Black	Dark Cordovan Metallic
Bright Bittersweet	Light Medium Blue
Bright Blue	Medium Blue Glow
Bright Caramel	Medium Gray Metallic
Bright Red	Polar White
Bright Yellow	Silver Metallic
Chamois Glow	

TU-TONE EXTERIOR COLOR COMBINATIONS

UPPER COLOR/LOWER COLOR

Bittersweet Glow/Dark Cordovan Metallic	Light Medium Blue/Bright Blue
Bright Bittersweet/Dark Cordovan Metallic	Polar White/Bittersweet Glow
Chamois Glow/Dark Chamois Metallic	Polar White/Bright Yellow
Dark Chamois Metallic/Chamois Glow	Silver Metallic/Dark Cordovan Metallic
Dark Cordovan Metallic/Bittersweet Glow	Silver Metallic/Medium Gray Metallic

ENGINE CODES

2.3L 2V 4 cyl 88 hp (MT)	A
2.3L 2V 4 cyl 90 hp (AT)	A
2.3L 2V 4 cyl (Turbocharged)	W
3.3L 1V 6 cyl 91 hp (MT)	B
3.3L 1V 6 cyl 94 hp (AT)	B
4.2L 2V V-8 119 hp	D

VEHICLE IDENTIFICATION NUMBERS

0	Last digit of model year
F	Assembly plant (F-Dearborn, R-San Jose)
02	Body code for coupe (03-hatchback, 04-Ghia, 05-hatchback Ghia)
A	Engine code
100001	Consecutive unit number

For example: 0F02A100001

1981

PRODUCTION FIGURES

Coupe	77,458
Coupe, Ghia	13,422
Hatchback	77,399
Hatchback, Ghia	14,273
Total	**182,552**

RETAIL PRICES

Coupe, standard	$5,897
Hatchback, standard	$6,566
Hatchback, Ghia, standard	$6,786

EXTERIOR COLORS

Black	Light Pewter Metallic
Bittersweet Glow	Medium Blue Glow
Bright Bittersweet	Medium Pewter Metallic
Bright Red	Midnight Blue Metallic
Bright Yellow	Pastel Chamois
Dark Brown Metallic	Polar White
Dark Cordovan Metallic	Red

TU-TONE EXTERIOR COLOR COMBINATIONS

UPPER COLOR/LOWER COLOR

Bittersweet Glow/Black	Medium Pewter Metallic/Light Pewter Metallic
Bright Bittersweet/Black	Pastel Chamois/Black
Bright Red/Black	Polar White/Bittersweet Glow
Bright Yellow/Black	
Dark Cordovan Metallic/Black	Polar White/Black
Light Pewter Metallic/Black	Red/Black
Medium Pewter Metallic/Black	Red/Polar White

ENGINE CODES

2.3L 2V 4 cyl 88 hp	A
3.3L 1V 8 cyl 94 hp	B
4.2L 2V V-8 120 hp	D

VEHICLE IDENTIFICATION NUMBERS

1FA	Ford Motor Co.
B	Restraint system (B-active belts)
P	Passenger car
10	Body code for coupe (15-hatchback, 12-Ghia coupe, 13-Ghia hatchback)
A	Engine code
6	Check digit which varies
B	Year (B-1981)
F	Plant (F-Dearborn)
000001	Consecutive unit number

For example: 1FABP10A6BF000001

1982

PRODUCTION FIGURES

Coupe	45,316
Coupe GLX	5,828
Hatchback	69,348
Hatchback GLX	9,926
Total	**130,418**

RETAIL PRICES

Coupe, standard	$6,346
Coupe, GLX, standard	$6,980
Hatchback, standard	$6,979
Hatchback, GLX, standard	$7,101

EXTERIOR COLORS

Bittersweet Glow	Medium Gray Metallic
Black	Medium Vanilla
Bright Red	Medium Yellow
Dark Blue Metallic	Pastel Vanilla
Dark Cordovan Metallic	Polar White
Dark Curry Brown Metallic	Red
Medium Blue Glow	Silver Metallic

TU-TONE EXTERIOR COLOR COMBINATIONS

UPPER COLOR/LOWER COLOR

Bittersweet Glow/Black	Medium Gray Metallic/
Bright Red/Black	Silver Metallic
Dark Blue Metallic/Black	Medium Vanilla/Black
Dark Blue Metallic/	Medium Vanilla/Pastel
Medium Blue Glow	Vanilla
Dark Cordovan Metallic/	Medium Yellow/Black
Bittersweet Glow	Pastel Vanilla/Black
Dark Cordovan Metallic/	Polar White/Black
Black	Red/Black
Medium Blue Glow/Black	Silver Metallic/Black
Medium Gray Metallic/	
Black	

ENGINE CODES

2.3L 2V 4 cyl 88 hp	A
3.3L 1V 6 cyl 94 hp	B
4.2L 2V V-8 120 hp	D
5.0L 2V V-8 157 hp	F

VEHICLE IDENTIFICATION NUMBERS

1FA	Ford Motor Co.
B	Restraint system (B-active belts)
P	Passenger car
10	Body code for coupe (16-hatchback, 12-coupe GLX, 13-hatchback GLX)
A	Engine code
6	Check digit which varies
C	Year (C-1982)
F	Plant (F-Dearborn)
000001	Consecutive unit number

For example: 1FABP10A6CF000001

1983

PRODUCTION FIGURES

Convertible	23,438
Coupe	33,201
Hatchback	64,234
Total	**120,873**

RETAIL PRICES

Convertible, standard	$12,467
Coupe, standard	$6,727
Hatchback, standard	$7,439

EXTERIOR COLORS

Black	Light Desert Tan
Bright Bittersweet	Medium Charcoal Metallic
Bright Red	Medium Yellow
Dark Academy Blue Metallic	Midnight Blue Metallic
Dark Walnut Metallic	Polar White
Desert Tan Glow	Red
Light Academy Blue Glow	Silver Metallic

ENGINE CODES

2.3L 1V 4 cyl 88 hp	A
2.3L EFI 4 cyl 145 hp (Turbo GT)	T
3.8L 2V V-6 112 hp	3
5.0L 4V V-8 176 hp (HO)	M

VEHICLE IDENTIFICATION NUMBERS

1FA	Ford Motor Co.
B	Restraint system (B-active belts)
P	Passenger car
26	Body code for coupe (27-convertible, 28-hatchback)
A	Engine code
6	Check digit which varies
D	Year (D-1983)
F	Assembly plant (F-Dearborn)
000001	Consecutive unit number

For example: 1FABP26A6DF000001

1984

PRODUCTION FIGURES

Convertible	17,600
Coupe	37,680
Hatchback	86,200
Total	**141,480**

PRODUCTION FIGURES
20TH ANNIVERSARY EDITION

Convertible Turbo GT	104
Convertible 5.0L GT	1,213
VIP Convertibles	16
Ford of Canada (total)	246
Hatchback 5.0L GT	3,333
Hatchback Turbo GT	350
Total	**5,262**

RETAIL PRICES

Convertible, standard	$11,840
Coupe, standard	$7,089
Hatchback, Standard	$7,260

EXTERIOR COLORS

Black	Light Academy Blue Glow
Bright Canyon Red	Light Desert Tan
Bright Copper Glow	Medium Canyon Red Glow
Dark Academy Blue Metallic	Oxford White
Dark Charcoal Metallic	Silver Metallic
Desert Tan Glow	

ENGINE CODES

2.3L 1V 4 cyl 88 hp	A
2.3L EFI 4 cyl 145 hp (Turbo GT)	T
2.3L EFI 4 cyl 175 hp (SVO)	W
3.8L EFI V-6 120 hp	3
5.0L EFI V-8 165 hp	F
5.0L 4V V-8 175 hp (HO)	M

VEHICLE IDENTIFICATION NUMBERS

1FA	Ford Motor Co.
B	Restraint system (B-active belts)
P	Passenger car
26	Body code for coupe (27-convertible, 28-hatchback)
A	Engine code
6	Check digit which varies
D	Year (D-1984)
F	Assembly plant (F-Dearborn)
000001	Consecutive unit number

For example: 1FABP26A6DF000001

1983 Hatchback

1985

PRODUCTION FIGURES

Convertible	15,110
Coupe	56,781
Hatchback	84,623
Total	**156,514**

RETAIL PRICES

Convertible, standard	$12,237
Coupe, standard	$6,989
Hatchback, standard	$7,509

EXTERIOR COLORS

Black	Oxford Gray
Canyon Red	Oxford White
Dark Sable	Pastel Regatta Blue
Jalapena Red	Sand Beige
Medium Charcoal	Silver
Medium Regatta Blue	

ENGINE CODES

2.3L 1V 4 cyl 88 hp	A
2.3L EFI 4 cyl 205 hp (SVO)	W
3.8L EFI V-6 120 hp	3
5.0L EFI/4V V-8 165/210hp (HO)	M

VEHICLE IDENTIFICATION NUMBERS

1FA	Ford Motor Co.
B	Restraint system (B-active belts)
P	Passenger car
27	Body code for convertible (26-coupe, 28-hatchback)
A	Engine code
6	Check digit which varies
F	Year (F-1985)
F	Assembly plant (F-Dearborn)
000001	Consecutive unit number

For example: 1FABP27A6FF000001

1986

PRODUCTION FIGURES

Convertible	22,946
Coupe	83,774
Hatchback	117,690
Total	**224,410**

RETAIL PRICES

Convertible, standard	$13,214
Coupe, standard	$7,420
Hatchback, standard	$7,974

EXTERIOR COLORS

Black	Light Regatta Blue Metallic
Bright Red	Medium Canyon Red Metallic
Dark Clove Metallic	Oxford White
Dark Gray Metallic	Sand Beige
Dark Sage	Shadow Blue Metallic
Dark Slate Metallic	Silver Metallic

ENGINE CODES

2.3L 1V 4 cyl 88 hp	S
2.3L EFI 4 cyl 205 hp (SVO)	W
3.8L EFI V-6 120 hp	3
5.0L EFI V-8 200 hp (HO)	M

VEHICLE IDENTIFICATION NUMBERS

1FA	Ford Motor Co.
B	Restraint system (B-active belts)
P	Passenger car
28	Body code for hatchback (26-coupe, 27-convertible)
A	Engine code
6	Check digit which varies
G	Year (G-1986)
F	Plant (F-Dearborn)
000001	Consecutive unit number

For example: 1FABP28A6GF000001

1987

PRODUCTION FIGURES

Convertible	32,074
Coupe	43,257
Hatchback	94,441
Total	**169,772**

RETAIL PRICES

Convertible, standard	$13,052
Coupe, standard	$8,271
Hatchback, standard	$8,690

EXTERIOR COLORS

Black	Medium Cabernet
Bright Regatta Blue Metallic	Medium Shadow Blue Metallic
Dark Clove Metallic	Medium Yellow
Dark Gray Metallic	Oxford White
Dark Shadow Blue Metallic	Sand Beige
Light Gray	Scarlet Red

ENGINE CODES

2.3L 1V 4 cyl 88 hp		A
5.0L EFI V-8 225 hp (HO)		M

VEHICLE IDENTIFICATION NUMBERS

1FA	Ford Motor Co.
B	Restraint system (B-active belts)
P	Passenger car
40	Body code for coupe LX (41-hatchback LX, 42-hatchback GT, 44-convertible LX, 45-convertible GT)
A	Engine code
6	Check digit which varies
H	Year (H-1987)
F	Plant (F-Dearborn)
000001	Consecutive unit number

For example: 1FABP40A6HF000001

1988

PRODUCTION FIGURES

Convertible	32,074
Coupe	53,221
Hatchback	125,930
Total	**211,225**

RETAIL PRICES

Convertible, standard	$13,702
Coupe, standard	$8,835
Hatchback, standard	$9,341

1987 GT Hatchback

EXTERIOR COLORS

Almond	Deep Shadow Blue Metallic
Black	Light Gray
Bright Red	Medium Shadow Blue
Bright Regatta Blue Metallic	Metallic
Cabernet Red	Oxford White
Dark Gray Metallic	Tropical Yellow

ENGINE CODES

2.3L 1V 4 cyl 88 hp		A
5.0L EFI V-8 225 hp (HO)		M

VEHICLE IDENTIFICATION NUMBERS

1FA	Ford Motor Co.
B	Restraint system (B-active belts)
P	Passenger car
40	Body code for coupe LX (41-hatchback LX, 42-hatchback GT, 44-convertible LX, 45-convertible GT)
A	Engine code
6	Check digit which varies
J	Year (J-1988)
F	Plant (F-Dearborn)
000001	Consecutive unit number

For example: 1FABP40A6JF000001

1989

PRODUCTION FIGURES

Convertible	42,244
Coupe	50,560
Hatchback	116,965
Total	**209,769**

RETAIL PRICES

Convertible, standard	$14,140
Coupe, standard	$9,050
Hatchback, standard	$9,556

EXTERIOR COLORS

Almond	Deep Shadow Blue Metallic
Black	Light Gray
Bright Red	Medium Shadow Blue Metallic
Bright Regatta Blue Metallic	Oxford White
Cabernet Red	Tropical Yellow
Dark Gray Metallic	

ENGINE CODES

2.3L 1V 4 cyl 88 hp		A
5.0L EFI V-8 225 hp (HO)		M

VEHICLE IDENTIFICATION NUMBERS

1FA	Ford Motor Co.
B	Restraint system (B-active belts)
P	Passenger car
44	Body code for coupe LX (41-hatchback LX, 42-hatchback GT, 44-convertible LX, 45-convertible GT)
A	Engine code
6	Check digit which varies
K	Year (K-1989)
F	Assembly plant (F-Dearborn)
000001	Consecutive unit number

For example: 1FABP44A6KF000001

1990

PRODUCTION FIGURES

Convertible	26,958
Coupe	22,503
Hatchback	78,728
Total	**128,189**

RETAIL PRICES

Convertible, standard	$14,810
Coupe, standard	$9,753
Hatchback, standard	$10,259

EXTERIOR COLORS

Black	Deep Titanium
Bright Red	Light Titanium
Bright Yellow	Oxford White
Cabernet Red	Twilight Blue
Crystal Blue	Wild Strawberry
Deep Emerald Green	

ENGINE CODES

2.3L EFI 4 cyl 88 hp		A
5.0L EFI V-8 225 hp (HO)		M

VEHICLE IDENTIFICATION NUMBERS

1FA	Ford Motor Co.
C	Restraint system (C-air bags and active belts)
P	Passenger car
40	Body code for coupe LX (41-hatchback LX, 42-hatchback GT, 44-convertible, 45-convertible GT)
A	Engine code
6	Check digit which varies
L	Year (L-1990)
F	Assembly plant (F-Dearborn)
000001	Consecutive unit number

For example: 1FACP40A6LF000001

1991

PRODUCTION FIGURES

Convertible	21,513
Coupe	19,447
Hatchback	57,777
Total	**98,737**

RETAIL PRICES

Convertible, standard	$16,767
Coupe, standard	$10,702
Hatchback, standard	$11,208

EXTERIOR COLORS

Black	Medium Titanium
Bright Red	Oxford White
Deep Emerald Green	Titanium Frost
Light Crystal Blue	Twilight Blue
Medium Red	Wild Strawberry

ENGINE CODES

2.3L EFI 4 cyl 105 hp		S
5.0L EFI V-8 225 hp (HO)		E

1991 Coupe

VEHICLE IDENTIFICATION NUMBERS

1FA	Ford Motor Co.
C	Restraint system (C-Air bags and active belts)
P	Passenger car
42	Body code for hatchback GT (40-coupe LX, 41-hatchback LX, 44-convertible, 45-convertible GT)
E	Engine code
6	Check digit which varies
M	Model year (M-1991)
F	Assembly plant (F-Dearborn)
000001	Consecutive unit number

For example: 1FACP42E6MF000001

1992

PRODUCTION FIGURES

Convertible	23,470
Coupe	15,717
Hatchback	40,093
Total	**79,280**

RETAIL PRICES

Convertible, standard	$16,899
Coupe, standard	$10,125
Hatchback, standard	$10,721

EXTERIOR COLORS

Bimini Blue	Oxford White
Black	Titanium Frost
Bright Red	Twilight Blue
Deep Emerald Green	Ultra Blue
Medium Red	Wild Strawberry
Medium Titanium	

ENGINE CODES

2.3L EFI 4 cyl 105 hp	S
5.0L EFI V-8 225 hp (HO)	E

VEHICLE IDENTIFICATION NUMBERS

1FA	Ford Motor Co.
C	Restraint system (C-air bags and active belts)
P	Passenger car
45	Body code for convertible GT (40-coupe LX, 41-hatchback LX, 42-hatchback GT, 44-convertible)
E	Engine code
6	Check digit which varies
N	Model year (N-1992)
F	Assembly plant (F-Dearborn)
000001	Consecutive unit number

For example: 1FACP45E6NF000001

1993

PRODUCTION FIGURES

Convertible	27,300
Coupe	24,851
Hatchback, standard	57,084
Hatchback, Cobra	4,993
Total	**114,228**

RETAIL PRICES

Convertible, standard	$17,988
Coupe, standard	$11,159
Hatchback, standard	$11,664

EXTERIOR COLORS

Black	Reef Blue
Bright Blue	Royal Blue
Bright Calypso Green	Silver
Bright Red	Vibrant White
Electric Red	

ENGINE CODES

2.3L EFI 4 cyl 105 hp	S
5.0L EFI V-8 205 hp (HO)	E
5.0L Cobra EFI 235 hp	D

VEHICLE IDENTIFICATION NUMBERS

1FA	Ford Motor Co.
C	Restraint system (C-air bags and active belts)
P	Passenger car
44	Body code for convertible (40-coupe, 41-hatchback LX, 42-hatchback GT, 45-convertible GT)
E	Engine code
6	Check digit which varies
P	Model year (P-1993)
F	Assembly plant (F-Dearborn)
000001	Consecutive unit number

For example: 1FACP44E6PF000001

1994

PRODUCTION FIGURES

Convertible, Cobra	1,000
Convertible, 3.8L	18,333
Convertible, GT	25,381
Coupe, Cobra	5,009
Coupe, GT	30,592
Coupe, 3.8L	42,883
Total	**123,198**

RETAIL PRICES

Convertible, standard	$20,160
Convertible, GT	$21,790
Convertible, Cobra	$25,605
Coupe, standard	$13,365
Coupe, GT	$17,280
Coupe, Cobra	$21,300

EXTERIOR COLORS

Black	Laser Red
Bright Blue	Opal Frost
Canary Yellow	Rio Red
Crystal White	Teal
Deep Forest Green	Vibrant Red
Iris	

ENGINE CODES

3.8L EFI V-6 145 hp	4
5.0L EFI V-8 215 hp	E
5.0L EFI V-8 240 hp	O

VEHICLE IDENTIFICATION NUMBERS

1FA	Ford Motor Co.
L	Restraint system (L-air bags and active belts)
P	Passenger car
40	Body code for coupe (42-coupe GT, 44-convertible, 45-convertible GT)
4	Engine code
6	Check digit which varies
R	Model year (R-1994)
F	Assembly plant (F-Dearborn)
000001	Consecutive unit number

For example: 1FALP4046RF000001

1995

PRODUCTION FIGURES

Convertible, standard	48,264
Convertible, Cobra	1,003
Coupe, standard	137,722
Coupe, Cobra	4,005
Total	**190,994**

RETAIL PRICES

Convertible, standard	$20,995
Convertible, Cobra	$25,605
Coupe, standard	$14,530
Coupe, Cobra	$21,300

EXTERIOR COLORS

Canary Yellow	Opal Frost
Black	Rio Red
Bright Blue	Sapphire Blue
Crystal White	Teal
Deep Forest Green	Vibrant Red
Laser Red	

ENGINE CODES

3.8L EFI V-6 145 hp	4
5.0L EFI V-8 215 hp	E
5.0L EFI V-8 240 hp	O
5.8L EFI V-8 300 hp	O

VEHICLE IDENTIFICATION NUMBERS

1FA	Ford Motor Co.
L	Restraint system (L-air bags and active belts)
P	Passenger car
45	Body code for convertible GT (40-coupe, 42-coupe GT, 44-convertible)
4	Engine code
6	Check digit which varies
S	Model year (S-1995)
F	Assembly plant (F-Dearborn)
000001	Consecutive unit number

For example: 1FALP4546SF000001

1996

PRODUCTION FIGURES

Convertible, standard	15,246
Convertible, Cobra	2,510
Convertible, GT	17,917
Coupe, standard	61,187
Coupe, Cobra	7,496
Coupe, GT	31,624
Total	**135,980**

RETAIL PRICES

Convertible, standard	$21,060
Convertible, Cobra	$27,580
Convertible, GT	$23,495
Coupe, standard	$15,180
Coupe, Cobra	$24,810
Coupe, GT	$17,610

EXTERIOR COLORS

Black	Mystic
Bright Tangerine	Pacific Green
Deep Forest Green	Rio Red
Deep Violet	Opal Frost
Laser Red	Crystal White
Moonlight Blue	

ENGINE CODES

3.8L EFI V-6 150 hp	4
4.6L SOHC EFI V-8 215 hp	W
4.6L DOHC EFI V-8 305 hp (SVT Cobra)	V

VEHICLE IDENTIFICATION NUMBERS

1FA	Ford Motor Co.
L	Restraint system (L-air bags and active belts)
P	Passenger car
40	Body code for coupe (42-coupe GT, 44-convertible, 45-convertible GT, 47-Cobra coupe, 46-Cobra convertible)
W	Engine code
6	Check digit which varies
T	Model year (T-1996)
F	Assembly plant (F-Dearborn)
000001	Consecutive unit number

For example: 1FALP40W6TF000001

1997

PRODUCTION FIGURES

Convertible, standard	11,606
Convertible, GT	11,413
Convertible, Cobra	3,088
Coupe, standard	56,812
Coupe, GT	18,464
Coupe, Cobra	6,961
Total	**108,344**

RETAIL PRICES

Convertible, standard	$21,280
Convertible, GT	$24,510
Convertible, Cobra	$28,135
Coupe, standard	$15,880
Coupe, GT	$18,525
Coupe, Cobra	$25,335

EXTERIOR COLORS

Autumn Orange	Deep Violet
Aztec Gold	Laser Red
Black	Moonlight Blue
Crystal White	Pacific Green
Deep Forest Green	Rio Red

ENGINE CODES

3.8L EFI V-6 150 hp	4
4.6L SOHC EFI V-8 215 hp	W
4.6L DOHC EFI V-8 305 hp	V

VEHICLE IDENTIFICATION NUMBERS

IFA	Ford Motor Co.
L	Restraint system (L-air bags and active belts)
P	Passenger car
45	Body code for convertible GT (40-coupe, 42-coupe GT, 46-convertible, 47-coupe)
W	Engine code
6	Check digit which varies
V	Model year (V-1997)
F	Assembly plant (F-Dearborn)
000001	Consecutive unit number

For example: 1FALP45W6VF000001

1997 Coupe

1998

PRODUCTION FIGURES

Convertible, standard	21,254
Convertible, GT	17,024
Convertible, Cobra	3,480
Coupe, standard	99,801
Coupe, GT	28,789
Coupe, Cobra	5,174
Total	**175,522**

RETAIL PRICES

Convertible, standard	$20,650
Convertible, GT	$24,150
Convertible, Cobra	$28,510
Coupe, standard	$16,150
Coupe, GT	$20,150
Coupe, Cobra	$25,710

EXTERIOR COLORS

Atlantic Blue	Dark Green Satin
Autumn Orange	Laser Red
Black	Pacific Green
Bright Atlantic Blue	Performance Red
Chrome Yellow	Rio Red
Crystal White	Silver

ENGINE CODES

3.8L EFI V-6 150 hp	4
4.6L SOHC EFI V-8 225 hp	W
4.6L DOHC EFI V-8 305 hp	V

VEHICLE IDENTIFICATION NUMBERS

1FA	Ford Motor Co.
L	Restraint system (L-air bags and active belts)
P	Passenger car
40	Body code for coupe (42-coupe GT, 44-convertible, 45-convertible GT, 46-Cobra convertible, 47-Cobra coupe)
W	Engine code
6	Check digit which varies
W	Model year (W-1998)
F	Assembly plant (F-Dearborn)
000001	Consecutive unit number

For example: 1FALP40W6WF000001

1999

PRODUCTION FIGURES

Convertible, standard	19,299
Convertible, GT	13,699
Convertible, Cobra	4,055
Coupe, standard	73,180
Coupe, GT	19,634
Coupe, Cobra	4,040
Total	**133,907**

RETAIL PRICES

Convertible, standard	$21,070
Convertible, GT	$24,870
Convertible, Cobra	$31,470
Coupe, standard	$16,470
Coupe, GT	$20,870
Coupe, Cobra	$27,470

EXTERIOR COLORS

Atlantic Blue	Electric Green
Black	Laser Red
Bright Atlantic Blue	Performance Red
Chrome Yellow	Rio Red
Crystal White	Silver
Dark Green Satin	

ENGINE CODES

3.8L EFI V-6 190 hp	4
4.6L SOHC EFI V-8 260 hp	W
4.6L DOHC EFI V-8 320 hp (SVT Cobra)	V

VEHICLE IDENTIFICATION NUMBERS

1FA	Ford Motor Co.
L	Restraint system (L-air bags and active belts)
P	Passenger car
42	Body code for coupe GT (40-coupe, 44-convertible, 45-convertible GT, 46-Cobra convertible, 47-Cobra coupe)
W	Engine code
6	Check digit which varies
X	Model year (X-1999)
F	Assembly plant (F-Dearborn)
000001	Consecutive unit number

For example: 1FALP42W6XF000001

1999 Cobra Coupe

2000

PRODUCTION FIGURES

Convertible, standard	41,368
Convertible, GT	20,224
Convertible, Cobra	100
Coupe, standard	121,026
Coupe, GT	32,321
Coupe, Cobra	354
Total	**215,393**

RETAIL PRICES

Convertible, standard	$21,370
Convertible, GT	$25,270
Convertible, Cobra	$31,605
Coupe, standard	$16,520
Coupe, GT	$21,015
Coupe, Cobra	$27,605

EXTERIOR COLORS

Amazon Green	Electric Green
Atlantic Blue	Laser Red
Black	Performance Red
Bright Atlantic Blue	Silver
Crystal White	Sunburst Gold

ENGINE CODES

3.8L EFI V-6 190 hp	4
4.6L SOHC EFI V-8 260 hp	W
4.6L DOHC EFI V-8 320 hp (SVT Cobra)	V
5.4L SOHC EFI V-8 (SVT Cobra "R")	H

VEHICLE IDENTIFICATION NUMBERS

1FA	Ford Motor Co.
L	Restraint system (L-air bags and active belts)
P	Passenger car
45	Body code for convertible GT (40-coupe, 42-coupe GT, 44-convertible, 46-Cobra convertible, 47-Cobra coupe)
W	Engine code
6	Check digit which varies
Y	Model year (Y-2000)
F	Assembly plant (F-Dearborn)
000001	Consecutive unit number

For example: 1FALP45W6YF000001

Index

Page numbers that appear in italics denote pages that show an illustration for the entry.

Further Reading

A Century of Automotive Style,
100 Years of American Car Design,
Michael Lamm and Dave Holls,
Lamm-Morada Publishing Company, Inc., 1996

Art of the American Automobile,
Nick Georgano, Smithmark Publishers Inc., 1995

Ford Mustang,
Mike Mueller, Motorbooks International, 1995

Mustang, Anniversary Edition 1964 – 1994,
Nicky Wright, Prion Books Ltd., 1996

Mustang,
Jim Campisano, Metro Books, 1997

Mustang,
Randy Leffingwell, Motorbooks International, 1995

Mustang 5.0 and 4.6,
Matt Stone, MBI Publishing Co., 1998

Mustang! The complete History of America's Pioneer Ponycar,
Gary L. Witzenburg, Princeton Publishing, Inc., 1979

Mustang Does It!,
Ray Miller, The Evergreen Press, 1997

Mustang Red Book, Third Edition,
Peter C. Sessler, MBI Publishing Co., 2000

Saleen, The History and Development of the Saleen Mustang,
Patty Redeker, California Mustang Sales and Parts, Inc., 1994

Shelby Mustang,
Tom Corcoran, MBI Publishing Co., 1992

Acknowledgments

This book is dedicated to the memory of Robert D. Negstad.

The author would like to thank: William Bozgan of Ford Motor Company, this book's technical editor and photo co-editor, whose knowledge of Ford products and ability to navigate the Ford Motor Company archives were invaluable; Mustang lover Elaine Dodson, who gave many hours of her time to help track down the Mustang owners whose cars were photographed; Tim Boyd of Ford Motor Company for additional technical review; Rebecca Benton, Molly Harrison, and Denise MacIntyre for editorial assistance; Jim LaRussa for graphic assistance; Tim Bollinger for technical data compilation; and for additional research, administrative, and photographic assistance Dan R. Erickson, Afaf Farah, Paula M. Lewis, Eugene Malymeik, Mose Nowland, Denise L. Skicki, and Nick Zuk.

Special thanks also to the Mustang owners who allowed their cars to be photographed or who supplied their photography: Steel Beam, 1991 coupe; Vernon Bush, 1965 Shelby; Bill Cabaniss, 1968 fastback; Larry Carr, pedal car; David Colley, 1969 Mach I; Bill Curvin, 1987 GT fastback; Mike Denton, 1967 Shelby GT500; Vickie Denton, 1966 convertible; Elaine Dodson, 1973 convertible; Johnny Dunn, 1968 convertible; Todd Greenwald, 1979 Pace Car, 1986 SVO fastback, 1996 SVT Cobra; Gary Hanson, 1966 T-5 fastback; Rick Harmon, 1968 convertible; Charles Hurliman, 1971 Mach I, 1983 GT fastback, 1969 Shelby GT500; Joe Ingarra, 1966 coupe; Shawn Johnston, 1969 coupe; Charles Landreth, 1968 Shelby GT500KR; Larry Maddox, 2000 Saleen; Patricia Martin, 1969 GT convertible; Dexter New, 1966 GT fastback; Dave Percy, California Special; Charles Ping, 1970 Boss 429, 1991 Saleen; Phil Schmidt, 1974 Mustang II and 1978 King Cobra; Bob Slocum, 1964$\frac{1}{2}$ convertible; Rod Tieszen, 1999 GT Anniversary coupe; Larry Vincent, 1966 Shelby GT350H. Thanks also to those who provided Mustang memorabilia to be photographed: Ross Davenport, JoAnne MacKinzie, Charles Ping, Phil Schmidt, Richard Skender, Mark and Dan Stacey, John Sullivan, Rod Tieszen, and Dave Young.

Picture Credits
Abbreviations: *b* = bottom, *t* = top, *c* = center, *l* = left, *r* = right.
Jacket photographs: (Front) Keith Harrelson (Back) **Ford Motor Company** *tl*; Keith Harrelson *tc, tr*; (Flaps) Keith Harrelson
Inside photographs: All photos courtesy of Ford Motor Company with the following exceptions: **Associated Press** 8, 10*t*; **Bandit Trans Am Club** 113*br*; **William Bozgan** 33*c*, 37*c*, 37*t*, 76*t*, 108*t*, 109*tr*, 127*tr*, 152*t*, 174*cl*; **Bettman/Corbis** 16*tr*, 16*bl*, 17*br*, 40*bl*, 97*tr*, 97*br*, 112*bc*, 112*br*, 113*bc*, 130*t*, 130*bc*, Henry Diltz 17*br*, Owen Franken 96*tr*, Wally McNamee 96*br*; **Hal Crocker** 12*t*, 150, 151*tr*, 151*l*, 151*br*, 157*bc*, 172*b*, 173*tr*, 173*c*, 173*br*; **Patrick Covert** 37*t*; **DK Picture Library**/Nick Goodall 36*t*, Matthew Ward 24, 25, 80*bl*, 86*tr*; **Dave Friedman** 54*t*, 55, 74*t*, 75*c*, 75*b*, 80*bc*, 81*t*, 83*t*, 83*c*; **Mike Genovese** 60*bl*; **Gary Hanson** 35*t*; **Keith Harrelson** 1, 3, 4, 5, 6, 7, 9, 13, 14, 15, 20*t*, 20*b*, 21*tl*, 21*tr*, 21*cr*, 26, 27*t*, 26*t*, 26*b*, 27*t*, 30, 31, 32, 33*t*, 36*b*, 37*b*, 37*c*, 38, 39, 41*bc*, 41*br*, 44, 45, 47*b*, 48, 49, 50, 51, 56, 57, 58, 59, 60*bc*, 64, 65, 66, 67*t*, 67*c*, 70, 71, 76*b*, 77, 81*bl*, 82, 83*br*, 84, 85, 86*b*, 87, 88, 89, 90, 91*br*, 92, 93, 94, 95, 100, 101, 106, 109*tl*, 109*c*, 110, 111, 116, 117, 118, 124, 126, 127*tl*, 127*c*, 128, 129, 131*t*, 131*bc*, 134, 135*tr*, 137*br*, 138, 139, 142, 143, 144, 145, 146*tl*, 146*b*, 148, 153*t*, 153*c*, 154, 155, 164, 165*tc*, 165*tr*, 167*br*, 168*b*, 169*br*, 171*br*, 174, 174*tl*, 174*c*; **Index Stock** 103*b*; **Indianapolis Motor Speedway** 130*bl*, 130*br*, 131*br*, 135*tl*, 156*bl*; **Rob Kurtycz** 172*t*, 173*tl*; **Dave Percy** 40*t*; *Time* magazine 16*tl*; **Mike Veglia**/Motor Sport Visions Photography, 173*tl*. **Illustration: David Kimble** 160.

NOTE: Every effort has been made to trace the copyright holders. DK Publishing apologizes for any unintentional omissions and would be pleased, in such cases, to add an acknowledgment in future editions.